ADVANCE PRAISE FOR
SERIAL KILLERS AND SADISTIC MURDERERS— UP CLOSE AND PERSONAL

"Power, control, attention, and social company—these are just a few of the insights Jack Levin provides in his latest work on 'up close and personal' murder in the United States. *Serial Killers and Sadistic Murderers—Up Close and Personal* is a necessary document for those interested in criminological analysis, detailed storytelling, and social problem solving. As Levin states in the introduction, he has 'paid the price' for doing what few people are willing to do—seriously pay attention to and dissect the motivations for serial killing. We, the readers, reap the benefits."

—Derek Pardue, cultural anthropologist at Washington University in St. Louis and editor of *Ruminations on Violence*

"Readers should appreciate the balanced approach that Dr. Levin brings to this grim, disturbing topic. He offers the reader a number of insights into the perplexing question of 'why do they do it?' He challenges us to go beyond common but often misinformed thinking in pursuing answers to this grim question. His discussions are analytical and insightful, but not devoid of emotion regarding the horrific deeds on which his research has focused. As he confesses, acquiring the information shared in this book has come at some personal cost."

—Dwayne Smith, PhD, professor, Department of Criminology University of South Florida

"It's a great read. With close to three decades of experience in the analysis of aberrant violent offenders, Professor Levin accomplishes a rare feat in offering the reader true insight to the perpetrators of some of the world's most hideous crimes."

—Richard N. Kocsis, PhD Forensic psychologist, author of *Criminal Profiling*

"I am frequently asked by attorneys, law enforcement officers, students, and private citizens about recommended readings and relevant literature pertaining to the topic of serial killers. Jack Levin's book *Serial Killers and Sadistic Murderers—Up Close and Personal* is a book that I will recommend to all those who want to study and understand the motives and behavior of these lethal predators."

—Alan C. Brantley, president of BCS International and FBI supervisory special agent/profiler (retired)

serial
killers
AND SADISTIC MURDERERS

Up Close and Personal

serial killers

AND SADISTIC MURDERERS

Up Close and Personal

JACK LEVIN

Prometheus Books

59 John Glenn Drive
Amherst, New York 14228-2119

Published 2008 by Prometheus Books

Inquiries should be addressed to
Prometheus Books
59 John Glenn Drive
Amherst, New York 14228–2119
VOICE: 716–691–0133, ext. 210
FAX: 716–691–0137
WWW.PROMETHEUSBOOKS.COM

12 11 10 09 08   5 4 3 2 1

Library of Congress Cataloging-in-Publication Data

Levin, Jack, 1941–
    Serial killers and sadistic murderers—up close and personal / Jack Levin
        p. cm.
    Includes bibliographical references and index.
    ISBN 978–1–59102–576–4
    1. Serial murders—Case studies. 2. Murderers—Case studies. 3. Murderers—Psychology. I. Title.

HV6515.L483 2008
364.152'30922—dc22

                                                                        2007051798

Printed in the United States on acid-free paper

To Flea, with love

CONTENTS

FOREWORD

As the cofounder of the FBI's Violent Criminal Apprehension Program, I have become aware over the years of the superb work that Jack Levin has done in analyzing the motives and methods involved in the most grotesque and hideous types of murder. His work in examining the behavior of serial killers, mass murderers, and other killers has been a significant contribution to the literature in criminology.

I found this book very interesting in that Levin melds his professional and personal insights on these killers into an engrossing and illuminating work. His personal and candid thoughts in regard to meeting such notorious murderers as the Hillside Strangler and speaking with Charles Manson, for example, shed new light on the actual thoughts that professionals have but rarely voice on their personal experiences in dealing with actual killers. Rather than leave the book wholly based on impressions, however, Levin soundly substantiates his assumptions with the cold facts of the case and his professional analyses of the types of killers and their motivations.

This is a book I would recommend to both the public and professionals in its balance of candid emotions and hard facts. Jack Levin has dedicated his life to the pursuit of understanding the elusive ways of killers and haters. What makes his work special is that he not only targets the issues and problems associated with understanding the minds of killers and then bringing them to justice, he suggests ways both to thwart them and to redirect the energies of budding killers. With Jack Levin as your guide, you are in the hands of a true expert.

Robert K. Ressler

ACKNOWLEDGMENTS

A number of individuals deserve to be recognized for their significant role in helping to produce this book. Terry Beadle at Northeastern University skillfully refined several of my photographs; Ben Cooley, who is an outstanding physician, answered my medical questions; Eleanor Pam provided insights into the Pamela Smart case; David Traub in the Norfolk County DA's office informed me about local cases; and Eric Madfis did a first-rate job of researching several of the cases depicted in the book. I also want to thank three undergraduate students at Northeastern—Sandra Hussey, Sarah Bakanosky, and Megan Krell—who were very helpful to me while serving their co-op positions at the Brudnick Center. I also thank Sarah Cope and Daniela Methe, who contributed a good deal as research assistants at the center.

My colleagues—especially Jack McDevitt Arnie Arluke, Denise Bissler, Tom Koenig, Gordana Rabrenovic, Michael Handel, Bob Gittens, and Sylvia Domínguez—were generous with their encouragement and constructive feedback. The contributions of James Alan (Jamie) Fox have been particularly important. Since the early 1980s, he and I have worked closely together, studying and writing about various types of murder. At this point, it is sometimes impossible to separate his ideas from mine. He also accompanied me to both Kingston and Walla Walla penitentiaries. I am deeply grateful.

Betty and the late Irving Brudnick have served as my mentors. Their encouragement and support have made possible an agenda of research in the areas of violence and hate that would have otherwise been out of the question.

Scott Wolfman and members of his talented team—Greg Bura, John O'Marra, and Sarah Rine—deserve much credit for educating college students as to the conditions associated with violence and hate.

In the area of multiple murder and related topics, I acknowledge the valuable work of Robert Ressler, Eric Hickey, Reid Meloy, Steve Egger, David Cantor, Kim Rossmo, Ron Holmes, Tom Fleming, Elliott Leyton, Elizabeth Englander, Richard Rappaport, Richard Kocsis, Kenna Quinet, Tom Cottle, Kay Gillespie, James McNamara, Michael Welner, Frederic Reamer, Gregory Sokolov, Ann Burgess, Alan Burgess, Roy Hazelwood, Brent Turvey, and Robert Keppel.

Finally, I recognize the contributions of the members of my wonderful family—my wife, Flea, and our children Michael, Bonnie and Brian (and now Benjamin), and Andrea and Mike (and now Jaden). They have provided the support and encouragement I needed to move through the stages of a project that demanded incredible amounts of time. I have always appreciated their tolerance, patience, and love.

Jack Levin
Boston, Massachusetts

INTRODUCTION

In the pages that follow, I relate my professional and personal experiences with serial killers and sadistic murderers. Drawing largely on firsthand encounters, I seek to make a number of points about the worst sorts of slayings in the form of lessons I have learned about murder as a criminologist who specializes in analyzing extreme violence and who has met, observed, and corresponded with a number of serial killers and other murderers—as well as their family members, neighbors, friends, lawyers, and victims (those few who were fortunate enough to escape).

Over the past twenty-five years, I have specialized in the study of murder, especially of the most irrational and despicable kinds. During this period, I have had many opportunities to examine the methods and mentality of brutal killers and other violent criminals. Thus, I have conducted face-to-face interviews and corresponded by mail and phone. I have also testified in criminal and civil court cases, consulted with prosecution and defense attorneys, and assisted the police in apprehending violent predators. Finally, I have often been asked to comment on newsworthy incidents of homicide for newspaper and television reporters.

The net result of my research into the motives, minds, and modus operandi of the murderer has taught me a number of significant lessons that I wish to share with readers. My personal experiences are, I hope, interesting in themselves, but they should also be useful for making some crucial points about the conditions under which the worst kinds of murder occur.

But I must confess from the outset that I have also paid a high personal price for my work in analyzing the most depraved of murderers. Over the years, I have received death threats from the fans of killers about whom I have written. I have gotten nasty letters and phone calls from strangers who judge me based only on a short quote (or mis-quote) in a newspaper article they've read. I have received letters from numerous prisoners who believe I might get them a new trial or a reduced sentence, mistakenly believing that I am an attorney rather than a criminologist. Mobsters have visited my office. Psychotics have stalked me. And I have viewed the most graphic crime scene photos, tapes of hideous tortures, and grisly autopsy reports.

The net result is that I have a broader perspective than I had twenty-five years ago, when I first decided to embark on a career in criminology. Immersing myself in so much death, danger, and destruc-tion, I also have a darker view of human nature now than before. But most disturbing of all, I am still sickened when I allow myself to think about the most ghastly crime scenes and victim dump sites I have encountered. And I have observed the results of the most inhumane sorts of murder: decapitations, eviscerations, dismemberments, sexual posing of bodies, and so on. To this day, it remains difficult to get a good night's sleep.

Living with murder has not always been easy. Yet by analyzing and better understanding—*not justifying*—the thoughts and actions of serial killers and other murderers, we can hopefully develop strategies that will thwart them and therefore benefit society. To the extent that we are successful, my experiences with murder will have been totally worthwhile.

Chapter 1

CONVERSING WITH THE DEVIL

By the time of my visit to Washington State's largest penitentiary in Walla Walla, Ken Bianchi had already served five years of his life sentence there. Along with his older cousin Angelo Buono, Bianchi had brutally tortured and killed ten girls and women in the Los Angeles area. And then, on his own, he relocated to Bellingham, Washington, where he murdered two more young women. While in partnership with his cousin, Bianchi had left virtually no physical evidence at the crime scenes. In fact, the police in Los Angeles suggested that the killing cousins must have scrubbed the walls and furniture in Angelo's upholstery shop where their victims had been tortured, because literally no fingerprints or other incriminating evidence could be found anywhere on the premises. Indeed, the fact that absolutely no fingerprints had been left on the walls, the furniture, or the glassware indicated that something was very wrong. This was not a normal living area. The killers had taken great pains to clean the crime scene.[1]

Operating alone in Bellingham, however, Bianchi was not as careful. Shortly after he arrived in Bellingham, the bodies of two female college students, Karen Mandic and Diane Wilder, were discovered in the back of an automobile off a highway in a wooded area of the city. They had been raped and murdered.

The two young women had been hired by Ken Bianchi, who was

working as a security guard for Coastal Security Company, to house-sit an upscale single-family home. It was in the Bayside neighbor-hood, and the alarm system was temporarily down.

Unlike his modus operandi with his cousin in Los Angeles, Bianchi left physical evidence that implicated him in the murders. At the crime scene in Bellingham, he left pubic hairs on the carpet. In his house, the police found blood- and semen-stained clothing, as well as Karen Mandic's phone number. Of course, the phone number alone wasn't much evidence because Bianchi had hired her, but all the evidence together pointed to him. Apparently, it was Angelo Buono who was the organized and careful member of the team. If Bianchi had killed without his partner in Los Angeles, he might have been caught without having amassed a large body count.

Bianchi was finally apprehended. As a result of a plea bargain, however, he was never tried in California and didn't get the death penalty. In exchange for a life sentence, he consented to cooperate with the prosecution in testifying against his cousin Angelo, who was convicted, sentenced to life, and later died of heart failure in his prison cell at Calipatria State Prison.

The state of Washington has had a number of high-profile slayings in addition to those perpetrated by Bianchi. After remaining on the loose for more than twenty years, fifty-three-year-old Gary Ridgway, aka the Green River Killer, was convicted of the brutal murders of forty-eight prostitutes in the Seattle area. A couple of decades earlier, Ted Bundy of Tacoma confessed to twenty-eight murders in states around the country, including Washington, and was executed in Old Sparky by the state of Florida. Near Vancouver, Washington, Westley Allan Dodd tortured and killed three boys over a ten-week period. Serial killer Robert Yates Jr. was found guilty of taking the lives of fifteen women in Spokane County. And John Allen Muhammad, a former resident of Tacoma and one of the so-called DC Snipers, was sentenced to die by the state of Virginia after his fatal shooting of ten people in and around Washington, DC. He also killed victims in Alabama, Louisiana, Georgia, Arizona, and his former residence, the state of Washington.

I met Ken Bianchi in a small visitors' room in the Walla Walla prison in 1987.[2] He was noticeably larger and more mature than he had appeared just after being apprehended in 1979. It was obvious from his muscular physique that, during his confinement, the Hillside Strangler—as Bianchi had come to be known—had taken full advantage of the exercise yard by pumping iron on a regular basis. He was now more than willing to talk—but only in the third-person plural. Like so many other killers, Bianchi continued to hope against hope that he would get a new trial, so he maintained his innocence. Speaking with me, he talked about the motives, methods, and personal characteristics of *serial killers in general* rather than about himself and the crimes he had perpetrated.

Bianchi and I shook hands. His grip was so tight that I grimaced in pain. I am convinced that he wanted to send me a message: *"Look Dr. Levin, you might have your PhD and all that, but as long as we are together in this room, I am in charge, I am in control . . . and don't you forget it!"* And this was the hand that had throttled the necks of numerous women.

Under normal circumstances, a hard handshake might indicate little if anything about the motivation of an individual. Many ordinary and decent people shake hands firmly. But it occurred to me immediately that Bianchi's excessively strong grip was another sign of just how much he craved power and control. He enjoyed inflicting pain and suffering—it made him feel superior. Bianchi's sadistic behavior with his victims expressed the same theme. And he had held the entire city of Los Angeles in the grip of terror for several months, as he tortured, raped, and sodomized his victims and then dumped their nude bodies on the hillsides surrounding the area. Almost everything he did, both large and small, was designed to enhance his feeling of superiority.

In the beginning of their killing spree, Bianchi and Buono strangled their victims. But over time, their taste for sadism became more and more intense. They required larger amounts of brutality in order to get high on killing, much like a drug addict who needs ever-larger quantities of heroin to stay high. Strangulation alone was no longer satisfying enough. They then began tying their victims to a chair in Angelo's upholstery shop, where they performed the most hideous acts—electrocuting them and injecting cleaning fluid into their veins to make them convulse. Enjoying the screams and the pleas for mercy, they shared a good laugh at the expense of their victims' suffering. And then, when he and his cousin Angelo had had their fun, Bianchi put his victims out of their misery by strangling them and dumping their lifeless bodies.

The cousins also modified their choice of victim. Bianchi and Buono began with a prostitute. But as their victim count mounted, they began to select younger middle-class girls who were riskier to abduct and more likely to be missed. Like so many other serial killers, Bianchi and Buono—"the Hillside Stranglers"—were feeling invincible. After all, though they had stayed on the loose for months, they were not even suspects on anybody's list. So they cut corners, took unnecessary risks, and got careless. And that is exactly how they were eventually apprehended, when Bianchi made a fatal mistake.

My visit with the Hillside Strangler gave me a lesson at the gut level. Bianchi's message of power and control definitely got through to me. After shaking hands, we sat across from one another at a small table. As soon as the security guard left the room and we were alone, my anxiety level soared. And I suddenly was on my best behavior. After all, I was about to interview a sadistic serial killer—a man who had mercilessly murdered his victims, and all for the sake of a thrill, the excitement, the sense of power that he received from perpetrating his heinous crimes.

On the other hand, Bianchi was cagey with me. He never confessed to the murders, never discussed the details of his crimes, but instead talked in the third person about serial killers generally. Yes, serial killers possess skills that other criminals seem to lack. Yes, serial killers may be manipulative. Yes, serial killers may be motivated to achieve a sense of power.

I am sure that Bianchi was hoping (against hope) to gain some advantage from the law—a new trial, a reduced sentence, better accommodations, even a pardon from the governor. Serial killers never give up. They manipulate their victims, they manipulate the public, they manipulate law enforcement, they manipulate the prison system when they are apprehended, and they even manipulate criminologists. On the other hand, it should be noted that Bianchi did admit to me that he had lied about statements he made to psychiatrists about his mother's abusive behavior. He said that he had been told that his insanity defense would stand a much better chance if he could indicate having been brutalized during childhood. It was at this point that Bianchi had invented the story about his mother's holding his hand over a hot stove as a punishment for stealing.

Police found a large number of books in Bianchi's Bellingham apartment that could have taught him how to act insane, feign being hypnotized, and behave as if he had multiple personalities. He had apparently read about criminal investigations, about *The Three Faces of Eve*, about hypnosis, about abnormal psychology, and about criminology. He had purchased a number of college diplomas through the mail that he hadn't earned—a PhD in psychology and a certificate of achievement confirming that he was educated as a medical doctor. He had fooled his common-law wife into thinking that he was working on his dissertation in psychology. She wondered about it, but believed every word. The Ken she lived with wouldn't have killed anyone; he was a trustworthy person, as far as she knew.[3]

Similarly, while awaiting trial, Bianchi was able to convince several young women that he was an innocent man; that they could save his life by falsely providing him with an alibi. The most extreme case was that of freelance writer Veronica Compton, who wrote to Bianchi asking for his critique of a screenplay she had written about a female serial killer. Before long, the twenty-something woman had fallen in love with Bianchi. During a visit together, the serial killer suggested to her a plan that he hoped would result in his exoneration. He placed some of his semen in a rubber glove that Compton would smuggle out of the prison. Bianchi asked the groupie to convince the authorities that the real serial killer was still on the loose, making Bianchi look totally free of guilt. Compton was supposed to kill a woman and leave Bianchi's sperm at the crime scene to suggest that the murder was sexually motivated. The technology wasn't what it is today, so the DNA could not have been traced back to Bianchi. How could Bianchi be guilty when the sexually motivated murders continued to occur while he was imprisoned? Amazingly, Compton did what she could to comply with Bianchi's request, although she failed in her attempt to strangle a twenty-six-year-old cocktail waitress in Bellingham. Compton was later convicted of attempted murder.[4]

Later, Bianchi was able to deceive several psychiatrists and psychologists—all experts in multiple personality and hypnosis—into believing that he was a genuine multiple personality. Under hypnosis, Ken became Steve, his alter ego, the sadistic personality within him. Bianchi told the expert witnesses that, as a young child, he created an imaginary playmate named Steve as a psychological defense against the severe abuse that had he received from his mother. Later on, Steve became permanently etched into Ken's personality.

Not believing Bianchi's story, one of the psychiatrists for the prosecution, Dr. Martin Orne, planted an idea with the defendant to see how he would react. Orne told Bianchi, in a casual conversation while he was in an awake state, that there are almost never only two personalities in someone suffering from multiple personality syndrome; there are usually at least three. During his next hypnotic session, another alter ego suddenly emerged, that of Billy. Bianchi had taken the bait.

Even more damning, the true origin of Ken's alter ego, Steve, finally emerged. While still in the Los Angeles area, Bianchi had pretended to be a clinical psychologist with an advanced degree. He placed an ad in the newspaper, looking for another psychologist with whom to share office space. He asked that applicants send him their résumés as well as their college transcripts. Bianchi received an answer from a young man named Thomas Steven Walker. Bianchi deleted Walker's name from the transcript and substituted his own. He later used the forged transcript to apply for various positions as a professional psychologist. He also took Walker's name "Steve" as his supposed alter ego. Thus, Steve turned out to be a product of Bianchi's scheming character, not his childhood fantasies.

The manipulative nature of a serial killer knows no bounds. Bianchi was so convincing that some prosecution experts continued to believe his story long after Bianchi's trial had ended and even after he was found guilty. Serial killers know how to play the game: they are masters of presentation of self; they are experts at managing an impression of themselves that they wish to be accepted by others. They typically look and act more like victims than villains.

By the time of my visit with Bianchi, his insanity plea had failed, and I am sure that he no longer believed that he had a reason to hide the truth—finally, it seemed obvious to most objective observers—though probably not to his dedicated groupies—that he was a malingerer as well as a sadistic killer. He had feigned multiple personalities and hypnosis to avoid conviction. Then, when his plea was denied, he could afford, in a practical sense, to help free his mother from the stigma of being regarded as an abusive parent. His mother's needs counted, but only when they did not interfere with satisfying his own needs.

I didn't learn much more about the Hillside Strangler from our conversation together. Accompanied by my colleague James Alan Fox, also a criminologist, I had already spoken with Bianchi's mother and had studied hundreds of pages of his medical records, which included his psychiatric history. Court testimony by expert witnesses in psychiatry and psychology also helped to illuminate the details of the case.

After I spent a couple of hours with Ken Bianchi, the security guard returned and offered to show me out. When I was secure in knowing that I was leaving and Bianchi was staying behind, I decided to pay him back for his painful handshake. As we parted company, I grabbed his hand to shake it and attempted to impose a hurtful grip—the same tight grasp that he had used on me when we met. Bianchi only laughed. He knew exactly what I was up to, what I had in mind, and he enjoyed humiliating me again. It was a flea on an elephant, it was like a ninety-nine-pound weakling (though I am heavier than ninety-nine pounds) trying to kick sand in the face of King Kong. Ken Bianchi was still in charge of things, and he let me know it.

Chapter 2

GAINING A SADISTIC THRILL

My visit with Ken Bianchi was only one of many encounters I've had with murderers. Over the past twenty-five years, I have interviewed killers and provided testimony to the courts. The practical and educational value of my personal experiences with homicide has given me some insight into the methods and motivations of dedicated killers who are bent on taking the lives of their fellow human beings.

One lesson I've learned is that *power and control are much more important motivations for the worst kinds of criminal violence than many people realize.* Certainly, many criminals kill for money or other economic advantage; others have a deadly version of a temper tantrum and, when frustrated, kill when they lose control of themselves. Yet there are also many murderers who take the lives of their victims simply to experience a rush of power and control, or to reestablish control they feel has been wrested from them. They may use sex as a vehicle, but their true intention is to determine the fates of their victims. They really seek to control others and to gain a sense of their own superiority. They decide who suffers and who does not. They decide who lives and who dies. They like playing God.

I have come to learn that it is frequently not enough for a killer to feel powerful for the period of time that he tortures and kills his victims. The feeling quickly dissipates, spurring him to up the ante—to plan for his next attack in order to re-create the momentary high that he experienced while being destructive. But many killers also have a desire to convince others of their strength and importance, to be widely regarded as powerful individuals. In my own field, we might want to think of violent crime as being motivated by money or jealousy or revenge, but we professionals sometimes underestimate the role played by the desire to be seen by our peers, by our community, by our country, as a strong and dominant human being.

Many of us, professionals and the public alike, became more aware of this motive in the late 1990s, when high school and middle school students around the country—who had felt ignored or humiliated by their peers—began gunning down their fellow students in the classrooms. They wanted desperately to be regarded as important rather than as the outsider looking in. Unfortunately, the necessity of publicizing sensational crimes also sends the wrong message to our alienated youngsters. In April 2007, a twenty-three-year-old Virginia Tech senior opened fire on campus, taking the lives of thirty-two of his schoolmates and instructors. Days later, NBC News received a packet of materials sent by the killer, including photographs portraying him with his weapons. It became obvious that he wanted to be seen as a dangerous and powerful person, not as someone who should be ignored or ridiculed.[1]

Criminologists became more aware of the need by serial killers to maintain an image of power and dominance when these murderers started writing to the press and taunting the police. San Francisco's Zodiac Killer wasn't the only murderer who wanted desperately to be a big shot, to feel in charge of things, to loom large in the eyes of others. Charles Manson recently told me with some pride that he was the most famous person in history. Another killer I interviewed claimed to have been the most prolific murderer who ever lived. And the BTK Killer (*bind*, *torture*, and *kill*), a middle-aged man in Wichita, Kansas, stayed on the loose for more than thirty years, killing innocent people. He felt so neglected and ignored by the media that he began writing to the police and to television reporters, which finally did him in. If he hadn't wanted so much to be a celebrity, he might still be on the loose.

Similarly, in 1995, when Timothy McVeigh blew up 168 men, women, and children at a federal building in Oklahoma City, Unabomber Ted Kaczynski began to feel ignored. Over the seventeen years he was sending bombs through the mail, there was plenty of publicity about him in the newspapers and on television. But then, all of a sudden, society's attention had turned elsewhere, and Kaczynski became jealous of all the publicity that was given to McVeigh. He phoned the FBI and claimed that he had planted a bomb at LAX. He hadn't, but his threat was effective enough to give him the attention that he craved.

We also became more aware of the desire for power when three white supremacists in Jasper, Texas, chained James Byrd, a black resident who had hitched a ride, to the back of their pickup truck and dragged him for almost three miles down a dirt road. For the first two miles, Byrd was alive and conscious, trying in desperation to survive by arching his back to avoid contact with the road. As the truck moved around a curve, Byrd's head hit a concrete culvert, and he was instantly decapitated. The FBI videotaped the three-mile stretch of road that had taken Byrd to his death and showed it to an audience of criminal justice professionals, including me. The first thing I noticed was a line down the middle of the road, separating the right from the left lane. But this was no painted divider; it was a line of the victim's blood.

Establishing control, as we've seen, is also of paramount importance to certain serial killers. Most of them lack the internal control necessary to stop them from committing murder for fun. In the absence of a conscience or of empathy, they take the lives of victims with moral impunity. That is what makes a sociopath—an absence of conscience or empathy. Control and dominance also motivate serial killers who have a sadistic need to inflict pain and suffering. To the extent that they torture and sodomize and dismember, they feel a sense of power, dominance, and control over the lives of their victims. Thus, for sadistic serial murderers, control is missing in their psyche but prevalent in their motivation.[2]

Mass murderers—those who slay a number of victims simultaneously in a single location—also have issues with control. They believe they have lost control and strive to re-gain it. In most mass killings, a catastrophic loss sets in motion the planning stage for the crime. The killer may have gone through a nasty separation or divorce, lost a great deal of money in the stock market, lost his job or his home, or lost his standing in the community. The lives of such individuals suddenly spiral out of control, resulting in a profound sense of personal tragedy. In order to once again be in charge, they eliminate the people they believe to be responsible for their miseries.

Criminologists explain some murderous behavior as occurring in a subculture of violence. In some rural areas of the Deep South, as well as in impoverished areas of major cities, violence is not only tolerated but approved of to protect dignity and pride. An individual who is "dissed" might respond by shooting or stabbing the disrespectful party. In this subculture, violence occurs around arguments between friends, rival gang members, or acquaintances. Respect is a rare commodity, and some will kill in order to ensure that it doesn't slip away.

Still, the subculture of violence does not provide a simple catchall to explain most multiple murders. First, areas of the country where this subculture predominates are also extremely impoverished. It may not be the local culture but the local poverty that promotes disproportionate violence. We cannot be sure. Second, these areas have relatively few mass and serial murders, even if they do have high rates of homicide generally. Mass and serial killings usually do not occur over arguments. They are premeditated—methodical and planned. And they are disproportionately likely in states such as California, Florida, Texas, Alaska, New York, and Illinois, where there are large numbers of strangers. Many residents are newcomers who have relocated hundreds, perhaps thousands of miles from home for the sake of a job, leaving their family and friends back in places like Omaha, Cleveland, or Hartford. And when they get to their destination, they are physically

and psychologically alone. They have no place to turn for encouragement and support, nobody to get them through the hard times. A very
few solve their problems in a sadistic and brutal manner. In some
cases, it is this absence of community that creates the conditions for
rampant psychopathologies to flourish.

But why do sociopaths—who often find themselves psychologically alone—engage in brutally torturing others? The term *sadism*,
which refers to the pleasure derived from inflicting pain, suffering,
and humiliation, originated in the behavior of nineteenth-century
Frenchman the Marquis de Sade. His writings were filled with offensive images of torture and suffering. Extreme acts of sadism speak to
the sociopath's need to have complete control over his victim. Of
course, there have been countless sadistic acts since the Marquis de
Sade and probably before.

Since the early years of the twenty-first century, sadism has
assumed a more prominent position in prime-time television and other
media in the United States. In the face of intense competition for sales
and ratings and eager to capture the largest possible share of the
market, TV producers have introduced more and more programs that
appeal to their audience's desire to witness the graphic pain and suffering of others.

Sadistic media fare seems to appeal widely to the needs of many
Americans who are desperate to feel good about themselves, even if it
occurs at somebody else's expense. Viewers are given an opportunity
to watch contestants, dramatic characters, and crime victims who are
humiliated, tortured, or killed. They may feel superior and strong,
laughing at the losers, sneering at the miserable, the downtrodden, and
the weak.

In the 1960s, parents and psychologists complained about a
growing tendency to present violence without consequences, a trend
that might have led young people to believe that violent behavior
caused little if any pain and suffering. Some forty years later, the
excessive depiction of victims' suffering through violence may not be
responsible for serial murder, but it may be desensitizing American

youth to the very real effects of destructive behavior. On popular prime-time programs, viewers are given a steady diet of shows that humiliate, embarrass, and torture. In the process, they learn that it is socially acceptable to enjoy the suffering of others.

Psychoanalyst Eric Fromm wrote that sadism was uniquely human, at least among the primates.[3] Chimpanzees might kill members of their own species for food or dominance, but not for the fun of it. There are no Ken Bianchis or Angelo Buonos among the great apes. According to Fromm, the sadistic impulse is learned. It becomes operative in societies where individual needs remain unmet and leaves many with a profound sense of powerlessness. Those individuals who feel excessively weak are therefore more likely to delight in the miseries of others. The sadistic impulse seems to arise out of frustrating life circumstances that gyrate out of control in individuals who are struggling to gain a sense of self-worth. Misery loves miserable company, and there are countless individuals who enjoy the pain and suffering of others.

In the face of corporate mergers, big government, and global connections, a growing number of Americans feel powerless to influence their own futures, let alone the course of events in the larger society. Even worse, after the September 11 attacks on America, more and more individuals felt helpless and vulnerable. Through sadistic media images, however, they can temporarily feel superior to the individuals being abused, tortured, or embarrassed on the tube. They may feel a sense of control that is no longer possible in everyday life.

In addition, masculinity in our society is deeply associated with physical strength and dominance over others. In order to feel powerful, men who wouldn't dream of killing anyone assert their authority in socially acceptable ways. For instance, they become authoritarian politicians who vociferously lobby for harsh law and order policies, top business executives who hire and fire on a whim, or tough-minded attorneys who "kill in the courtroom" with their caustic words. As a result, popular culture is now rife with sadistic images. Stand-up comics often aim their savage barbs at the most vulnerable among us—the elderly, the infirm, the marginalized, and alienated—rather than at those in the uppermost echelons of government, entertainment, or business. What is considered "edgy" can be downright mean-spirited and cruel.[4]

It has become more and more common for contemporary television programs to depict the physical anguish of helpless victims in dramatic series as well as the emotional humiliation of ordinary people on so-called reality television shows. Representing the former, prime-time series such as *Vanished*, *24*, *Prison Break*, and *Criminal Minds* realistically depict extreme forms of torture being performed by either protagonists (Jack Bauer of *24*) or villains (usually serial killers or terrorists).

As for humiliation, a number of reality programs score high ratings by embarrassing ordinary people. In episodes of NBC's long-running prime-time program *Fear Factor*, contestants engage in a series of humiliating tasks. They are given electric shocks; are forced to swallow something they find disgusting, for example, sheep testicles, worms, cockroaches, live beetles; or are buried in a tank full of scorpions, rats, or spiders. If they fail to meet the "challenge," they are eliminated. If they succeed, they move on to face the next horrific task. The contestant who completes all required tasks wins the game.

The WB network's now defunct *Superstar USA*, where "only the bad survive," also thrived on sadism. In what looked like a parody of *American Idol*, the worst singers on *Superstar USA* were deceived into believing that they had won the contest because of their superior voices. At the end of the game, they were then informed that the "winners" were actually the biggest losers—those contestants who couldn't carry a tune.

Apparently taking its cue from *Superstar*, Fox's *American Idol* now spends week after week showing the worst possible singers, most of whom are absolutely incredulous when they are rejected from the competition. In the process, the vast television audience is provided with a cheap laugh at the expense of the most insecure, naive, and delusional contestants. Moreover, judge Simon Cowell's unsparingly blunt criticism of contestants on *American Idol* has made him a super-star celebrity in his own right. The same can be said for Donald Trump on *The Apprentice* ("You're fired!") and, for a time, Anne Robinson on *The Weakest Link* ("You *are* the weakest link. Good-bye!").

Some killers simply possess much more of the same need for sadism that is found in a less dangerous form in the general population. Although watching *24* might not make us torturers, we are likely being desensitized to extreme cruelty. Sociopaths, on the other hand, up the ante, craving increasingly more intense forms of sadism to feel satisfied. Bianchi's incredibly hard handshake is a tepid example of sadism, to be sure. But the craving for power and control has led some criminals, including Bianchi, to do much worse: to annihilate their families, sexually intimidate strangers, shoot their classmates or coworkers, dismember human bodies, and torture and kill their innocent victims.

John Wayne Gacy, for example, a man who murdered thirty-three boys and men in suburban Chicago was severely abused by a domineering father who beat him and his mother. Ultimately, Gacy identified with his aggressive father and grew up to crave power. His next-door neighbor explained to me that Gacy dominated a conversation, dominated his wife, and dominated his victims. He was obsessed with a need to control the course of each and every situation in which he participated.

And when they are not killing, serial killers find other ways to feel in charge. While on the loose, they might play a cat and mouse game with the police, taunting them with messages sent through the mail or left at crime scenes. David Berkowitz, aka Son of Sam, killed six people in New York City. While he was on the loose, Berkowitz sent letters to columnist Jimmy Breslin at the *New York Daily News*, which contained cryptic clues as to his identity. In Wichita, Kansas, Dennis Rader, the BTK Killer, mailed the police and reporters a number of word puzzles in which clues to his identity were embedded. San Francisco's Zodiac Killer, who took the lives of at least six and perhaps as many as sixty, was never caught, though he sent complex astrological clues to the police. The DC Snipers—John Muhammad and Lee Malvo—who terrorized the Washington, DC, area, shooting ten innocent people to death—left taunting messages at their crime scenes.

Taunting law enforcement is one way to feel powerful. Another is to spread fear and terror throughout a community, if not an entire nation, and become infamous in the process. Thus, serial killers enjoy making the cover of a celebrity magazine, tabloid news shows, or the evening news. They want to be given a moniker—a notorious name—that will ensure that their evil deeds are permanently embedded in our collective memory, that they become a household word. They want to read about themselves in the newspaper and watch the results of their escapades on television.

The press often complies by creating a moniker that is widely known—Son of Sam, Hillside Strangler, Tarot Card Killer, Unabomber, Sunset Strip Killer, Gainesville Ripper, Beast of BC, Cannibal Killer, Killer Clown, and so on. Some killers provide their own moniker, just to make sure that they have one. "BTK" was created by Dennis Rader, who, apparently desperate to go down in infamy, not only wanted to make sure that he was not forgotten but exhibited himself as the ultimate control freak by creating his own alias.

Not all serial killers are motivated by sadism. A few of them have been inspired by the profit motive. Dorothea Puente, a Sacramento landlady, murdered nine of her elderly tenants in order to steal their Social Security checks. Aileen Wuornos, the prostitute whose life was portrayed in the film *Monster*, killed seven men who picked her up as she hitchhiked across Route 95 in South Florida. Her motive? To steal their money. And the DC Snipers, Lee Malvo and John Muhammad, who shot to death ten people at random during a three-week period in October 2002, were hoping to extort $10 million from authorities in exchange for ending their killing spree. Their murders were apparently not motivated by race, because their victims came from different racial backgrounds.

Other serial killers seek a sympathetic response from their associates. Mary Beth Tinning, a mother in Schenectady, New York, suffocated nine of her infants, one at a time. Doctors thought the children all had a genetic disorder that resulted in Sudden Infant Death Syndrome, or SIDS. Actually, Mary Beth killed in order to gain the sympathy of her friends and relatives. After each death, she was showered with compassionate attention from those who attended her child's funeral and visited the grieving mother at home. Individuals who inflict injury on themselves to get attention from others suffer from a disorder known as Munchausen syndrome. Psychiatrists viewed Tinning's disorder as Munchausen by Proxy, whereby a parent inflicts injury on her children rather than herself. Mary Beth Tinning used her children's deaths to gain a sympathetic response from the members of her community.

For the Hillside Strangler and many other serial killers, sadistic murder represents the one and only means that they have for being in charge and gaining a sense of superiority over others. They are not interested in getting sympathy. They consider their moments spent inflicting pain and suffering as their greatest accomplishments, perhaps their only endeavors that have given them some sense of being successful. Apparently, they are unable to achieve what they desire in a legitimate, mainstream manner, so they go beyond what is considered proper and moral. Moreover, they are able to feel that sense of accomplishment only through murder.

Many serial killers are so thrilled with their murders that they keep mementos or souvenirs from their victims. Jeffrey Dahmer, who killed seventeen men and boys in Milwaukee, collected photographs of his victims' remains and body parts, which he kept in his refrigerator. Long Island prostitute slayer Joel Rifkin collected the jewelry and underwear of his victims. Robert Berdella of Kansas City kept detailed records of his tortures, describing the types and quantity of poisons he had administered to his victims, the length of time it took for his victims to succumb, and the symptoms they suffered before death. Danny Rolling, who murdered five college students in Gainesville, Florida, excised the nipples of his female victims and carried them off in a small plastic bag.

Most serial killers suffered profoundly during childhood. They may have been abused, sexually molested, or abandoned, and they learned to take out their anger on others. Animal abuse of a certain kind is common among budding sadistic killers. Shooting birds from a distance with a BB gun or killing game with a rifle would not appeal to a serial killer. Many serial killers begin their sadistic practices at a young age by torturing and killing domestic animals like dogs and cats. They kill someone's family pet or another animal that has been humanized in the culture. Their cruelty is usually hands-on, up close and personal, providing them with a feeling of control and power. Their torturing of a "family member" may ease their own feeling of vulnerability and powerlessness, but the pain and suffering they inflict also serves as a rehearsal for the sadistic human violence they will perpetrate years later.

After being beaten senseless by his mother, for example, eight-year-old Carroll Edward Cole strangled the family's puppy. Later that day, he drowned one of his friends who had been teasing him about his first name. Later in his life, Cole went on to strangle sixteen women in several states. Jeffrey Dahmer, at the age of ten, collected and dissected roadkill. As an older child, he killed cats in order to skin them and soak their bones in acid. Edmund Kemper burned the family's pet cat and then cut off its head. As a ten-year-old child, Henry Lee Lucas stabbed a calf in the neck and then had sex with it as it was dying. He raped dogs and cats. And he skinned alive a number of small animals. At the age of eleven, Arthur Shawcross beat and killed farm animals. During childhood, Clifford Olson smothered to death two pet rabbits. Albert DeSalvo, who many people believe was the Boston Strangler, trapped house pets—dogs and cats—in wooden crates and shot them with a bow and arrow. Serial killer Cesar Barone once tossed neighborhood cats into a closet with a monkey, in order to watch the monkey tear apart somebody's family pet. As a child, Lee Malvo, the younger of the two DC Snipers, repeatedly killed stray cats by shooting marbles at them with his slingshot. There are reports that he killed his own cat. It is interesting that Malvo was never "hands-on" in his choice of a weapon for ending the lives of his victims, whether they were cats or human beings. In both cases, he distanced himself from his targets. By contrast, the sexually sadistic murderers were more likely to choose an intimate method—stabbing, strangling, or bludgeoning—their animal victims.

Sociologist Arnold Arluke and I studied 154 individuals who had committed serious acts of animal cruelty.[5] As a comparison group, we also studied their next-door neighbors—usually very similar in terms of their socioeconomic status—who had not committed any known animal abuse. We found that those who perpetrated animal cruelty were five times more likely than their neighbors to commit acts of human violence—rape, assault, and even murder, four times more likely to commit property offenses, and three times more likely to commit drug offenses. In sum, animal abusers were significantly more likely to engage in a range of antisocial behaviors.

Enduring childhood misery alone does not, however, turn youngsters into serial killers, but it does leave them with a profound sense of powerlessness. Serial killers may be compensating for the inferior role they were forced to play during childhood. Killing gives them everything missing from their otherwise drab, dreary, and mundane existence. Rather than be just an ordinary person with ordinary talents and ordinary abilities, serial killers see themselves as becoming supermen who cannot be stopped by the police or the FBI. They often do outsmart the authorities to stay on the streets long enough to amass a huge body count. They are often beyond the suspicion of the law; or if they become suspects, they are adept at convincing others of their own innocence.

It is interesting indeed that so many serial and mass murderers do not begin killing people until they are in their middle years—in their thirties, forties, or fifties. If early childhood or genetics were exclusively to blame, we might expect these killers to become violent much earlier in life—when they are twelve or seventeen or twenty-two. The fact that they wait so long may indicate that they have more trouble than most people making the transition into adulthood and middle age.

At the very time they believe they should be reaching the pinnacle of success, they find instead that they are sliding downhill fast.

Most individuals who were abused and neglected as children learn to deal with their past and become decent, law-abiding citizens who have a keen sense of morality. But a few do not. Instead, they continue to suffer; they continue to be miserable. Unable to engage in any meaningful relationships, they continue drifting from place to place, person to person, and, eventually, victim to victim.

Danny Rolling is an example of such a person. I spent a good deal of time studying the murders he carried out in Gainesville, Florida.[6] Danny Rolling never killed anyone when he was a teenager or young adult, but he eventually became a killing machine. At the age of thirty-six, he murdered eight people, three in Shreveport, Louisiana, where he was born and raised, and then, eight months later, five more in Gainesville. During this period, he also shot his father in the face, taking out one of his eyes, but not finishing the job. His father survived. Rolling's murders in Gainesville were as brutal as they get. Five beautiful college students, four young women and one young man, all stabbed multiple times. One decapitated. With this victim, the killer cleaned up and positioned her severed head on a bookshelf for the shock value. The women were raped, their bodies were then draped over the edge of their bedspreads in a mockingly romantic pose. The male victim was stabbed forty-eight times and eviscerated.

The crime scene photos of Rolling's bloodied and dismembered victims' bodies were among the most hideous I have ever viewed. They were so offensive that I still cannot think of them in any detail without experiencing nightmares for several days.

Growing up, Rolling was abused, both physically and verbally, by his father. But the pain and suffering he experienced didn't end with adulthood. He had a short marriage and a nasty divorce. He couldn't hold a job. He got into arguments and fights. He couldn't get along with anybody. He drifted from Louisiana, ending up in one prison after another. He repeatedly committed burglary, auto theft, armed robbery, and assault. When he eventually got to Gainesville, he turned his rage on five innocent college students at the University of Florida.

Children who are abused are slightly more likely than others to become murderers. But only a small percentage of abused children do become killers, and an even tinier proportion end up as a Danny Rolling.

Chapter 3

SILENCING THE LAMBS

Clifford Olson is arguably the most notorious killer in Canadian history, though most Americans have never heard of him. It is entirely understandable, because culture travels north, east, and west from the United States. Most Canadians are familiar with the names Jeffrey Dahmer and Charles Manson. But Americans know little if anything about infamous killers among their neighbors to the north.

Olson was a construction worker who lived in British Columbia with his wife and son. Between jobs, he went to prison for committing such crimes as theft, fraud, armed robbery, obstruction of justice, possession of stolen property, firearm possession, forgery, breaking and entering, impaired driving, and escape from lawful custody. By the time of his forty-first birthday, Olson had spent only four years of his adult life outside of prison walls.

In his spare time, Olson raped and murdered children. In November 1980, he kidnapped a twelve-year-old girl in Surrey, British Columbia, whom he then strangled with a belt and stabbed repeatedly. In April 1981, he abducted a thirteen-year-old girl by luring her into his car, drugging her, raping her, and then beating her to death with a hammer. Also in April, he kidnapped a sixteen-year-old boy, bashing in his head with a hammer and tossing his body into a ditch by the side of the road. In May, only four days after his wedding, Olson gave a ride to a sixteen-year-old girl who was hitchhiking home. He took her

into the woods and beat her to death. In June, Olson murdered a thirteen-year-old girl whose brother and sister-in-law lived in his apartment complex. In July 1981, he kidnapped a nine-year-old boy and
strangled him to death. Also in July, he strangled a fourteen-year-old
girl to whom he had offered a ride. But first he drugged and raped her.
During the same month, Olson lured a fifteen-year-old boy into his car
and drove him to a campground, where he beat the boy to death with
a rock. Days later, Olson raped and beat to death an eighteen-year-old
German tourist and he lured a fifteen-year-old girl into his car on the
promise of a job. Once inside his automobile, Olson drugged, raped,
and then strangled the youngster. Olson's final act of homicide in July
was his murder of a seventeen-year-old girl in a gravel pit, where he
beat her to death with a hammer and buried her body in a shallow
grave.[1]

All told, Olson raped and murdered eleven children and teenagers,
eight girls and three boys, all in British Columbia. The fact that the
victims were of various ages and both female and male delayed the
police in realizing that one person was responsible for all the crimes.
At first, they believed that several child killers were on the loose.

The problem of recognizing a set of murders as the work of the
same perpetrator is widespread among homicide investigators, so
much so that criminologist Steven Egger at the University of Houston,
Clear Lake, gave it a name—*linkage blindness*.[2] When homicides
occur in different jurisdictions, the problem of linkage blindness
becomes particularly acute. Lack of communication among police
departments may obscure the fact that the murders being committed
over a broad area are indeed connected. But even when the killings are
perpetrated within a confined area, investigators may not connect the
dots. They may look in vain for a consistent modus operandi or victim
characteristics—always stabbing or strangulation, always older
female victims, always gay men. In reality, serial killers often vary the
characteristics they select in their targets, their time of day for stalking
victims, their method of killing, and so on. The immutable patterns
that many people expect to find in a serial killer exist only in the

mythology. Many serial killers vary their methods and types of victims to get away with murder for as long as possible or to prevent boredom from setting in.

The Royal Canadian Mounties were initially at a loss to establish credible suspects for the growing list of unsolved rape/murders of youngsters in British Columbia. When they finally realized that one serial killer was likely operating in the local area, they turned their attention to Clifford Olson. He had a lengthy criminal record and was regarded as a suspect. In August 1981, the police caught Olson giving a ride to a female hitchhiker. Rather than wait for him to kill again, they arrested Olson on a minor traffic charge and discovered that he was carrying an address book containing the name of one of the murdered victims.

Olson really believed that the Mounties had enough evidence to convict him, so when they offered him an unusual deal, he couldn't refuse. He was paid $100,000 in trust for his wife and son in exchange for leading the police to the unrecovered bodies of his victims. Not only did this agreement provide the authorities with the evidence they needed to convict Olson, but it also helped to ease the suffering of the victims' families, who were looking for some sense of closure.[3]

In January 1982, Olson pleaded guilty to eleven counts of murder and was given eleven life sentences. In July 2006, he was denied parole.

In the visitors' room at Ontario's Kingston Penitentiary, I spoke at length with serial killer Clifford Olson.[4] The diminutive killer referred to himself as the Beast of British Columbia.

In an effort to exaggerate what he considered his greatest accomplishments—the taking of human life, Olson bragged to me about murders I knew he could not possibly have committed. The famous character in Thomas Harris's book *The Silence of the Lambs* was his role model—except that Hannibal Lecter was only a figment of Thomas Harris's imagination, while Olson was very much real. He compared himself to Hannibal Lecter but saw himself as something far bigger and better. He was the ultimate serial killer.

Not unlike Lecter's fictional prison chamber, Olson's cell was covered by a Plexiglas shield containing a slot for his food. But, unlike the cinematic version, which was constructed in order to protect Lecter's visitors from harm, the purpose of Olson's shield was to stop other inmates from walking by and urinating on him. In prison culture, child killers and snitches are located at the lowest rung of the status hierarchy. And because he was both, Olson was positioned among the lowest of the low, someone the other inmates would be anxious to disassociate with or even to eliminate.

I wondered whether Olson was really a pure sociopath, a man without any semblance of conscience, morality, or superego. While speaking with him, I suddenly asked, "Cliff, you admit having murdered eleven children, yet you apparently never harmed your wife and son. Why not? Why did you not hurt or even kill them too?" Olson thought a while and finally replied. He told me that his wife and son respected him, and so he would not have any reason to harm them. At no point was he able to come up with the word *love* to explain why his family members were off-limits—not even to impress me. The word *love* was simply not part of his vocabulary.

Reinforcing the notion that Olson was a pure sociopath who lacked the capacity for remorse or empathy, parents of some of Olson's unfortunate victims came forward to say that the killer had later sent letters to them, describing the tortures in detail and explaining how much fun it had been killing their children. At one point, Olson was permitted by prison authorities to make a series of videotapes in which he described in gory detail the horrendous acts he had perpetrated on his victims, including hammering nails into their heads and then asking them how it felt.

Olson is as manipulative as any serial killer has ever been, desiring to be renowned for his evil deeds. To this day, after twenty-five years in prison, he has shown no remorse for his crimes. Instead, he now claims to have taken up to two hundred lives and says he would like to kill again. In July 2006, a jury denied Olson's request for parole.[5]

Olson and I kept in touch by phone for six months following my visit. He called me every Tuesday (collect, of course) on his cellular phone from his cell. During this period, I was teaching a course in criminal homicide to a large group of students. I asked my students to write the serial killer and ask him any questions they might have about his crimes or the crimes of others. Olson was very helpful. He answered hundreds of questions from my students in great detail. I think he enjoyed himself, though clearly that was not my purpose.

When Olson became a management problem, the Canadian authorities moved him from prison to prison. Just a month ago, I tried reestablishing contact with the serial killer. Unfortunately, the prison authorities refused to allow me to have anything to do with him. In fact, they would not even let him know that I had attempted to contact him. I could understand such measures if I were a tabloid reporter or someone who might stir up the prison population against the killer. But to prohibit my correspondence or visit is an excessive measure that would surely not occur in most prisons in the United States, except under the most extreme circumstances. Only by studying these monsters can we hope to understand how they think, how they develop, how to stop them, and how to possibly prevent them from reaching the point of becoming sadistic murderers.

Chapter 4

LOOKING MORE INNOCENT THAN AN INNOCENT MAN

For those who practice sexual sadism, power is achieved by inflicting pain and suffering. Of course, it is possible for a killer to have a power trip without using sex as a vehicle. At least a few hospital and other medical workers—typically holding marginal or powerless positions in the healthcare profession—have suffocated or poisoned their patients for a similar motive—in order to play God in deciding who lives and dies. A physician in England may have been responsible for poisoning to death several hundred of his patients. A Cincinnati orderly murdered sixty elderly patients. A nursing home administrator in Orkdal, Norway, poisoned to death 155 patients. A nurse in western Massachusetts took the lives of as many as forty hospital patients.

Television is mainly a medium meant for reporting, not conducting, research. Yet the ubiquitous presence of television talk shows, especially during the 1990s—*Geraldo*, *Sally Jesse*, *Jenny*, *Leeza*, *Jerry*, *Ricki*, *Rolanda*, *Oprah*, and the like—provided numerous opportunities for criminologists to interview individuals to whom they might otherwise never have been granted access. For some of these individuals—and perhaps for some professionals (not me)—the credibility of television and in some cases the lure of making money were an enticement to travel to New York, Chicago, or Los Angeles and expose themselves to the ridicule of a hostile audience and talk show host. Some obscure guests sincerely believed that they would be discovered by a producer or an agent and be flown off to Hollywood, where they would become stars of stage, screen, or television. But many went home totally stigmatized for the revelations about their deviant behavior, which they gladly, and naively, made to an audience of millions.

I first met thirty-eight-year-old Orville Lynn Majors in 1997 while taping an episode of *The Montel Williams Show*.[1] The focus of the program was on individuals falsely accused of crimes, and Majors was a featured guest. He had been a nurse in the intensive care unit at Vermillion County Hospital in Clinton, Indiana, a small facility containing fifty-six beds. In his twenty-two months working at the hospital, 147 patients died, most of them while Majors was on the job. In 1995, a supervisor at the hospital became suspicious of Majors when she noticed that the death rate increased in the intensive care unit during his shift and decreased again when the male nurse was off the unit.

Majors was suspended with pay, while the authorities exhumed seven bodies without finding any evidence of foul play. Montel's audience applauded in support when the male nurse suggested about his patients, "I am 100 percent certain I took care of these people and never hurt them."

Majors came dressed in a suit and tie. His brown hair and mustache were appropriately trimmed. And he was accompanied by his attorney, L. Marshall Pinkus, who voiced confidence that his client was an innocent man. The tension in the program was provided by several women who appeared on air to suggest that their older relatives had died mysteriously in the hospital on Majors's shift. They were convinced that the male nurse had murdered their loved ones. They said they had seen Majors administer a medication immediately before the patient expired; they observed Majors in proximity to a patient immediately before he died unexpectedly.

According to Majors, the suspicions about his role in the deaths of hospital patients was nothing short of "a nightmare." He told Montel that the accusations about his complicity in the mysterious deaths had "destroyed [him] and [his] family both mentally and financially."

Montel raised the possibility that the fact that Majors was gay might have kept the allegations focused on him rather than on other staff members. But Majors never saw his sexual orientation as an issue. He refused to place the blame elsewhere. He never suggested that his sexual orientation contributed to the allegations against him. Still, pure and simple: he was an innocent man.

My role on the program was simply to explain that once someone like Majors has been labeled a suspect, he is more likely to be regarded as guilty in the court of public opinion. Thus, every idiosyncrasy of the suspect that was formerly overlooked is made public, causing individuals who know him now to recognize every characteristic as a warning sign. They now think: he was strange, he acted bizarrely, he had an evil smile, he had temper tantrums, he was a loner, he once saw a psychiatrist, he had an emotionless blank stare, he was a weird fellow. Of course, prior to officially labeling the person as a possible killer, the same characteristics easily passed for normal. But once someone becomes a suspect in a murder case, everybody who knew him is transformed into a psychologist, recognizing all of the red flags and warning signs that had been missed beforehand.

After speaking with Majors in the green room and hearing what he had to say on air, I was convinced that Majors was an innocent man. And apparently so was Montel Williams, who may have seemed more sympathetic to the male nurse than to the family members of the victims. Montel pointed out that none of the families' accusations had been substantiated, that Majors had not been officially charged with any crime, and that Majors had basically "been raped" in the press.

The talk show host brought up the sixty lawsuits that had targeted the hospital as well as Majors after 140 patients died in the ICU where

Majors was employed. Williams wondered why it had taken two years for family members to decide to initiate these suits. Where was the evidence that their loved ones had been murdered? Where was the evidence that Majors had been involved? If they were so sure of his guilt, why hadn't the relatives acted immediately after the unexpected deaths to initiate their suits? Montel asked family members about allegations directed against Majors. "When you find out you were wrong, will you step up and help this man get a job, because he isn't going to get one as a nurse." The audience applauded sympathetically in support of the male nurse who they agreed was an innocent man, a victim of injustice.

His attorney reinforced the idea that Majors had been victimized. He told the audience that he had been completely comfortable allowing the male nurse to stay in his home with his wife and young children. Pinkus offered the following observation: "If I had any thought that he [Majors] had caused any death, he would not be in my home."

Here is what Montel and his audience failed to take into consideration. Hospitals are extremely vulnerable when a number of unexplained deaths have occurred. It is simply terrible public relations: who would want to be treated at a facility where a number of patients have mysteriously died?

Moreover, how do you prove that someone on a hospital staff—a nurse, a nurse's aide, an orderly, or even a doctor—has committed murder? After all, patients do die on the operating table or in recovery. Many patients are suffering from serious, even life-threatening illnesses. When a frail and sickly patient suddenly stops breathing, it may not be possible to determine definitively whether he died of natural causes or was suffocated with a pillow. And poisons inserted into a patient's IV may be impossible to detect, even upon autopsy. Indeed, it may never occur to anyone—staff members or loved ones alike—that the patient was murdered. Then, why bother to investigate? How do you succeed in confirming foul play even if you do suspect it? Why open a can of worms that could easily end in a humiliating defeat in court and the closing of the entire hospital?

In December 1997, Majors was arrested and charged with the murders of seven patients. These were the seven cases for which the prosecution had the strongest evidence. During his trial, Majors's benign façade was stripped away. A former roommate, Andy Harris, testified that the male nurse had told him he hated old people and said that "they should all be gassed."

Exhuming fifteen more bodies, investigators discovered that at least six deaths were attributable to poisonings by injections of epinephrine and potassium chloride. The murdered patients, four women and two men aged fifty-six to eighty-nine, died between 1993 and 1995. In the end, Majors was actually linked to at least 130 deaths: patients who died unexpectedly on Majors's shift or were seen close to him prior to their death. Some of the injections were witnessed by family members who had visited loved ones in the hospital. The son of one victim said about Majors: "I saw him inject my dad in the heart area, and my dad passed away within a minute or so, that quick." Vials of both drugs—epinephrine and potassium chloride—were found in Majors's home and van.[2]

On October 17, 1999, Majors was found guilty of six counts of premeditated murder and sentenced to serve 360 years. He will not be eligible for parole for at least 180 years. Montel Williams should have an updated program featuring suspects whom he had believed to be innocent on the first show but who were actually guilty.

Speaking with Majors and others like him, I've learned that *serial killers are expert at managing the impression they want us to accept of them.* They look so benign, so decent, so innocent. They seem beyond suspicion.

Orville Lynn Majors was perceived as more of a victim than a villain. He had been abused by the system, robbed of the job that he loved, accused of crimes he said he had never committed. Montel Williams was convinced that Majors was an innocent man. So was the audience. So was I.

Perhaps no serial killer exhibited the ability to appear innocent better than John Wayne Gacy, the owner of a construction company in suburban Chicago. In his spare time, Gacy kept busy torturing and murdering thirty-three men and boys. Gacy had been voted Jaycee Man of the Year. He was a big shot in local Democratic politics and he played a clown at children's parties. His neighbors considered him a terrific guy. One of them continued to visit Gacy on death row, long after his conviction on thirty-three counts of murder.

I spoke with Gacy's neighbor Lillian Grexa when she was in Boston for a couple of days.[3] When I asked why she would not abandon her relationship with Gacy, knowing that he was a prolific serial killer, Grexa explained that she knew him only as a good neighbor, not a deranged murderer. Human beings have an infinite capacity for compartmentalization.

Actually, Grexa had had a personal run-in with Gacy, but she still refused to reject him as a person. She explained to me that Gacy would hire sixteen- and seventeen-year-old boys to work for his construction company. At one point, her teenage son asked him for a job. Not only was he hired, he was also propositioned by the killer clown to have sex with him. You might think that this would have been the last straw for Grexa, who was being pressured by the press, public opinion, and neighborhood gossip.

Grexa admitted being "a little suspicious about Gacy's sexual preference" but not about whether he was a killer. When I asked whether she ever noticed any suspicious activities at Gacy's house next door, she was quick to point out that her house was located some twenty feet from his, separated by a large hedge that prevented her and her husband from seeing over it and into Gacy's residence.

But Grexa told me that her husband had once observed a rather strange occurrence in Gacy's yard. Ed Grexa came home from work one day and spotted Gacy standing chest-deep in a big hole in his yard. Grexa asked his neighbor what he was doing. He indicated that it looked as if he were digging a grave. Indignantly, Gacy responded: "Ed, what a thing to say to me. I am only putting in a barbeque pit. That's all." Well, an investigation later revealed that Gacy had buried one of the bodies under his barbeque pit. Even so, Lillian continued to write to Gacy on death row until he was executed. She told me, "I wrote John and asked him whether he would like to be my pen pal. I don't like what he did, but I like the man."

Another example of a brutal multiple murderer who was able to easily conceal his evil nature was Andrew Cunanan, the San Diego native who killed five people including designer Gianni Versace. He apparently had a face that reminded people of nobody in particular, which made him blend in with countless others walking the streets or driving their cars of any city, USA. Like so many other serial killers, he really had no features to distinguish him as an evil character. Instead, he looked like one of the boys, maybe the boy next door.

In 1997, Cunanan managed to remain a fugitive for more than two months while FBI agents and local law enforcement searched in vain to locate him. First, he murdered two men in Minneapolis. But before the local police even knew they had a double homicide on their hands, Cunanan was already in Chicago, killing again. And before the Chicago police got wind of his latest murder, he was already in south New Jersey, shooting a stranger in the head and stealing his red pick-up truck. Then, for two months, he got completely lost.

There were rumors that Cunanan was in drag, that he was wearing a series of disguises, that he had cleverly concealed his true identity. He was seen at the same time in San Diego, California; Chicago, Illinois; Lebanon, New Hampshire; four counties in North Carolina; and Naples, Florida. Actually, he was in Miami walking the streets, eating in restaurants, talking with strangers, and, eventually, walking past Versace's house and shooting him in the head. And he never wore a disguise, because it was totally unnecessary to do so.

Dennis Rader, the BTK Killer, was another serial killer who just didn't look like the monster that he was. He was able to avoid apprehension *for three decades*, killing ten innocent people and getting caught only when he resumed sending various items through the mail to the police and members of the press. His hobby was killing; his full-time position was a compliance officer who enforced the rules around the neighborhood. There were locals who might have thought badly of his rather rough-and-tumble style, but they never dreamed he was killing in his spare time. He seemed to be a man who valued the law—even excessively.

Orville Lynn Majors, the male nurse who killed at least six and as many as 130 hospital patients similarly didn't stand out, at least not in his appearance or demeanor. Even though family members of the victims suspected him, it took the authorities years before they were able to gather the evidence that would prove him guilty. Two years after his appearance on *The Montel Williams Show*, the licensed practical nurse ran out of luck and into a competent jury. He was finally tried and convicted of having poisoned his victims over a thirteen-month period at the Vermillion County Hospital in Clinton, Indiana, ninety miles west of Indianapolis.

Several years ago, I was in New York City, where I met Amy (a pseudonym), a ten-year-old girl from a small town in Ohio who considered Richard Ramirez, aka "the Night Stalker," to be a decent and honorable human being.[4] The twenty-seven-year-old serial killer was on death row in California when Amy and her grandmother established their friendship with him by mail, corresponding with him over a period of time. Ramirez's crimes were even more brutal than merely taking the lives of innocent people. In the dead of night, he broke into a number of single-family homes where he slashed the throats of his victims, sexually assaulted some of them, and then dismembered their bodies.

Amy was a sensitive girl who seemed to be lacking in friends among her peers and had bonded with her grandmother in their shared friendship with a serial killer. Amy showed me a doll that Ramirez had sent her as a token of his affection. She considered the killer a good friend, perhaps the only good friend she had. Her grandmother defended their mutual interest in the killer, suggesting that they both were able to see the goodness in him.

The Night Stalker wrote the following letter to Amy:

Hi sweetheart. I got your letter today. Always good to hear from you. You know how to read and write very well, huh? . . . I wish I could keep you and your grandmother company tonight, but they say I've been a bad boy, but its [*sic*] not true. . . . You and I will meet someday soon. Don't worry, there is plenty of time. . . . Tell me about school and who your favorite teacher is. Have you made any new friends? I miss talking to you on the phone. Maybe someday you can live near by [*sic*] so we can visit. If there is anything I can get for you, just let me know. Oh, I am sure there is nothing you need. But as always, your friend. Love you, Richard.[5]

Chapter 5

KILLING WITHOUT A CARE

Another lesson I have learned over the years involves the personality disorder known as sociopathy (or psychopathy). Many killers lack a conscience; they have no empathy for the pain and suffering of their victims (or, even worse, they might feel their victims' pain as their own pleasure). They care exclusively for their own pleasures in life and see other people merely as instruments to satisfy their personal desires, regardless of how perverse or reprehensible those desires may be. *Sociopaths (or psychopaths) are never remorseful when they do the wrong thing. They can therefore kill with moral impunity.*

In 1995, I testified in the penalty phase of the trial of serial killer Cesar Barone in Hillsboro, Oregon. It was clear to me that Barone lacked any feelings of compassion or empathy. He killed strangers, but he also assaulted intimates. He killed older women, but he also murdered younger women. In fact, he loved taking lives so much that given the chance, he might have killed anything that moved. There was nothing in his psyche to stop him. The only common denominator among his victims was their gender—all of them were females.

One expert suggested that he was trying to eliminate his mother, who had separated from his father when he was only four.[1] Perhaps Barone was compensating for feelings of abandonment that he had felt

from an early age. But his murderous intentions do not seem to be a
result of childhood abuse or neglect. Following his parents' divorce,
he apparently grew up in a decent, abuse-free home, where his stepmother cared about him and his father spent considerable time taking
him hunting, fishing, camping, and golfing.

In 1976, when he was fifteen years old, Barone broke into the
home of seventy-year-old Alice Stock, a retired schoolteacher and resident of Fort Lauderdale, Florida. He threatened her with a knife and
ordered her to remove her clothing, but he never actually attacked her
or harmed her physically. Stock was nevertheless terrified. She
reported the incident to the police and was able to identify Barone as
her attacker. As a result, the teenager served a sentence of two months
and eleven days in the Florida Department of Youth Services at its
Okeechobee School for Boys. Three years later, however, he went
back to Stock's residence to finish what he had started. This time, he
raped and strangled the elderly woman to death.

While authorities were still searching for Alice Stock's killer,
Barone was grieving the loss of his older brother, who had died in an
automobile accident. Three weeks later, he sexually assaulted and
attempted to strangle the stepmother who had raised him. Not wanting
to go through the ordeal of a courtroom proceeding, she never reported
the rape to the police, and Barone was never punished for it. A few
months later, he was arrested for allegedly attempting to strangle his
grandmother but was acquitted of that charge a short time later.[2]

In 1987, after moving from Florida to Oregon where he continued
in his murderous ways, Barone legally took the name that he would
use for the rest of his years. In Florida, he was content to use his birth
name, Adolph James Rode. But in Oregon, he changed his ethnic identity in keeping with his admiration for his "Italian heritage" and used
the name Cesar Francesco Barone. Another significant change in his
life occurred after relocating to the Northwest. He married Kathi
Lockhart, an attractive thirty-two-year-old woman from Seattle with
whom he corresponded after meeting her through a personal ad she
had placed in the local newspaper. The happy couple found an ideal

setting for their early years together in the picturesque town of Hillsboro, Oregon.

While living in the community of Hillsboro, Barone was responsible for four more deaths.

In April 1991, he sexually assaulted and strangled a sixty-one-year-old woman in her Hillsboro home.

In October 1992, he shot and killed a forty-one-year-old nurse-midwife who was on her way home from delivering a baby when Barone sprayed her car with bullets. He then attempted to rape the injured woman but ended up dragging her into the street and shooting her in the head.

In December 1992, Barone shot to death a twenty-three-year-old woman after attempting to rape her. He then dumped her body off the side of a highway.

In January 1993, he was responsible for the death of a fifty-one-year-old woman in her apartment. After having some drinks together, Barone followed his victim into the bathroom where he sexually forced himself on her, causing her to have a heart attack. To conceal his complicity, Barone then pushed her body into the bathtub, making it appear as though she had drowned while filling the tub.[3]

On January 27, 1995, I testified in Judge McElligott's courtroom during the penalty phase of the Martha Bryant murder trial. Bryant was the nurse-midwife whom Barone shot to death in October 1992 after attempting to rape her. Barone had already been convicted of first-degree murder. It was now up to the jury to decide between two alternative sentences: execution or life without parole eligibility.

In court, defense attorney Griffith Steinke began by questioning me about my research in the area of serial murder and then gave a biographical sketch of Barone's life history and his murders. Steinke reminded the court that the defendant had been convicted of killing Martha Bryant and was soon to be tried for the murders of Margaret Schmidt, Betty Williams, and Chantee Woodman. Barone had also been indicted in Florida for murdering Alice Stock.

Before addressing the issue of how the defendant should be sentenced, I was asked first to summarize the research I had conducted on serial killers by interviewing them, their wives and mothers, and their friends and neighbors. In my testimony on behalf of the convicted defendant, I argued that the court should keep Barone alive in order to study him. To prevent more serial murders in the future, I suggested, we need to do research on the Cesar Barones of the world, men who are pure sociopaths and who have taken a number of lives. Sparing this serial killer's life might lead us to better understand potentially dangerous individuals and prevent them from turning their rage into sadistic murder.

I then noted that it was not always easy to gain access to serial killers to study them. Many are awaiting execution and hoping for a reprieve, a new trial, or a commutation of their sentence. The last thing they want (or what their lawyers want) is to cooperate with a researcher by giving an honest account of the crimes they have perpetrated. Even if they were willing to be interviewed, they have every reason to lie. There were no grounds for expecting that Cesar Barone would be any different.

Steinke then questioned me as to whether a serial killer who serves a life sentence would be more cooperative and honest. I responded by suggesting that lifers are more willing to speak candidly because they do not see a need to save their life. They may have accepted a fate that they regard as impossible to change. At least they have their lives, even if they also have life sentences. In my own experience, lifers tend to be vastly more forthcoming than their counterparts on death row.

The defense attorney also asked me to estimate the prevalence of serial murder. I answered that it was extremely rare, representing less than 1 percent of all the homicides committed in the United States. Every year, approximately twenty serial killers are responsible for approximately two hundred victims. Though this number is too large and must be reduced, it pales by comparison with the fifteen thousand single-victim homicides committed annually. Thus, we are talking about a small number of killers who are responsible for a very large body count—on average, each killer takes the lives of ten people—

someone's daughter, someone's son, someone's mother, someone's father, someone's good friend.

Because of the sensationalistic nature of the crime, serial murders always make the headlines and the national news. I mentioned to the courtroom that their visibility therefore has a disproportionate impact on the public's thinking about violent crime and the effectiveness of the criminal justice system. The publicity given to serial murder also influences the general level of fear in society. When a serial killer is on the loose, almost everyone is scared, especially if his victims were normal, law-abiding citizens. Individuals feel vulnerable; anybody could be next.

I also suggested to the jury that what we learn from studying serial killers might help us understand more mundane crimes as well. Indeed, serial killing gives us an opportunity to examine mainstream America. In particular, I argued that "a lot of what motivates serial killers also motivates kids in the inner cities and kids in small towns who are going out on a Saturday night and, for the thrill and excitement, bashing people, assaulting people. Twenty years ago, they might have stolen hubcaps. Now they go out in a group looking for someone to attack or maybe to murder." Steinke asked me about patterns in the modus operandi of a serial killer. He addressed the issue in light of the fact that Barone had killed in a variety of ways, using several different kinds of weapons and going after various sorts of victims.

I pointed out that serial killers are not always as consistent and predictable as we would like them to be. The overwhelming majority kill strangers, but there are exceptions. Barone had killed both strangers and people he knew. The overwhelming majority kill by themselves, but Barone, in one case, had a partner. In four instances, he operated alone. Actually, the defendant's victims had only one common denominator—all of them were women.

Following the pioneering work of FBI profiler Robert Ressler and his colleagues, criminologists distinguish between "organized" and "disorganized" murderers. The disorganized killers are usually caught quickly. They may suffer from an extreme mental illness that makes them confused and unable to plan. They tend to act in a spontaneous manner, approaching the crime scene without taking precautions to avoid eyewitnesses and leaving the crime scene without bothering to clean it or to dump the bodies.

Most serial killers who stay on the loose for any period of time are, by contrast, organized, but not Barone. He never used restraints (e.g., handcuffs or tape) on his victims, he didn't dump the bodies, he didn't clean the crime scene, and he never waited for the optimal moment to strike so as not to be seen by eyewitnesses.

Moreover, unlike most other serial murderers, Barone used a gun on at least a couple of occasions. Killing with a firearm is generally a last choice in weaponry for a sadistic serial murderer. He wants the physical contact with his victim. He loves using his own hands. His victim's pain becomes his own pleasure.

The serial killer's inordinate desire for control and domination came up in my testimony: "They enjoy squeezing the last gasp of breath from their dying victims' bodies. They love hearing their victims scream and beg for mercy. That's precisely why they torture, rape, and kill. It makes them feel superior."

I added, "On almost every count, when talking about whether Barone used a partner or not, whether he targets strangers or not, whether he is organized or disorganized, whether he was abused or not, or whether he used a firearm, Barone does not fit any patterns. He is very rare among a rare breed. He didn't do anything that you would expect an organized serial killer to do . . . I haven't seen too many like Barone, I'll tell you." It is his very failure to conform to criminologists' expectations about serial killers that makes him such a valuable research subject.

As a final comment, I tried to convince the jury that we desperately need to understand better the variables implicated in the development of serial killers. The lesson is clear: "We're in the dark," I suggested. "We need to understand where this horrible phenomenon comes from so we can prevent it."

At first, I believed that the jury hadn't agreed with my argument.

Notwithstanding my testimony, Barone was given the death penalty and is presently on death row, awaiting execution. But defense attorney Steinke mentioned to me, after the sentencing decision came down, that the jurors really had accepted my testimony. They were convinced of the need to do research on killers like Barone, and they believed that he would be difficult if not impossible to examine while on death row.

But they were also convinced that Cesar Barone would never be executed. The State of Oregon hadn't carried out the death penalty on anyone since 1997. And the interval between sentencing and execution (when they were taking place) was very long—more than eight years. Jurors, like those who have voted for the death penalty, would likely lose track of the killers by the time they were actually executed. So, why not vote to kill a despicable serial killer? Why not send a message of law and order? Barone would never be executed anyway. The question left unanswered in my mind was how many defendants have been executed because jurors were convinced incorrectly that the death penalty is hardly ever carried out?

On Monday, January 1995, Cesar Barone was sentenced to death. In September 1998, he appealed his death sentence to the Supreme Court of the State of Oregon. Among his many challenges, the defendant contended that one of the juror's support for the death penalty was so extreme that she would automatically vote for execution no matter what the mitigating circumstances were. If so, then the defendant's right to an impartial jury was violated.[4]

In his appeal, Barone's defense team pointed to the following exchange between a juror and the defense attorney during the discovery phase of the trial:

Q: [defense attorney]: Are you of the opinion that everybody who commits that kind of aggravated murder like Ted Bundy should be put to death?

A: [juror]: I believe, when you get a personality type such as Ted Bundy's, there is virtually no chance for rehabilitation. I believe, yes, they should be executed. I don't believe the American public should have to support them. They serve no constructive good for society.

Q: Do you understand what I mean by aggravated murder? I mean something that is intentional and has an aggravating factor that's done with it like in the course of committing another crime.

A: Yes.

Q: Can you think of any situation, intentional murder that has those kinds of aggravating circumstances, can you think of any situation where the death penalty is not appropriate?

A: Not really.

Q: The fourth question is simply should the defendant receive a sentence of death. I want to ask it this way. If you get to this point in trial, as a juror, you would have already found a person guilty of intentional aggravated murder. You'd have already found that the person acted deliberately. Already found that there was no provocation, and you would have already found that there was a probability that that person would commit acts of violence in the future. With all that as background, is there any situation in which you could sentence or respond no to the question should a defendant receive a sentence of death?

A: I can't think of any.

Q: So, in every situation where those facts were in existence, you would answer yes to that question?

A: Yes, I would.

Q: Would it matter to you if the defendant there had a terrible childhood, had been abused, and neglected, and mistreated?

A: There is a lot of people who have that that don't go out and do these things.

Q: So that would not mitigate against the death penalty, if all those other things were answered yes?

A: No.

Q: What about the age of the person, what if there were someone who were eighteen, or nineteen, or fifty-five, or sixty or sixty-five, that wouldn't matter to you either?

A: No, it wouldn't.

Q: What if you were instructed by the judge to consider age, emotional pressure, things of that nature?

A: I would follow what the judge would tell me to do even though I might not agree with it.

Q: How can you follow that if you just told me that you would vote yes in every instance to that question?

A: Well, if the court dictates that you're supposed to do something, you know, they told me I was supposed to be here today, I'm here, you know.

Q: Is it one of those situations where you consider it and then vote yes?

A: I would probably, if the judge said we need to consider it, I would probably try to weigh the severity of it, okay? I mean, how bad was it?

Q: What would you do with that information? You just said you can't imagine voting anything but yes to that fourth question.

A: I know. I can't, you know. It would be extremely difficult for me because it would be something that is against everything I believe.

The defendant also highlighted the following exchange during discovery:

Q: [defense attorney]: Part of [your] belief system is that you resent, just quoting from your questionnaire, "resent supporting violent offenders that are of no use to society"?

A: [juror]: That's right.

Q: With that as part of your belief system, how can you ever answer no to question 4?

A: Like I said, I don't know that I could.

Q: Given what you've just told me, what do you think about life without the possibility of parole?

A: I've thought about that a lot, Okay. I guess in an aggravated murder case such as the definition you just gave me, I guess I ask why? I mean, why should this person continue in a situation where any kind of local tax dollars go on supporting that guy, you know, or gal, or whoever it may be? It makes no sense to me.

Q: Is that another reason to vote for the death penalty in every case of intentional, aggravated murder?"

A: Yeah.

The court of appeals affirmed the original judgment of conviction and Barone's sentence of death. His appeal was denied.[5]

In February 2007, I tried getting in touch with Cesar Barone on death row for the purpose of asking him a few unanswered questions about the murders he had committed. As though to confirm my contention that condemned inmates resist being studied, he refused to cooperate with me. It's difficult enough for dedicated criminologists and psychologists to have access to these killers, when they receive life sentences. Now we will probably never know what was going on in Barone's warped mind.

Chapter 6

HATING ENOUGH TO KILL

Hate crimes are perpetrated against those individuals considered "different," in terms of race, religion, national origin, sexual orientation, disability, status, or gender. In a number of cities and towns around the country, homeless people have recently been attacked by groups of teenagers. In six states, this also qualifies officially as a hate crime.

Power often plays a role in the motivation of a hate crime, just as it does in sadistic serial murder. The majority of such hate offenses are what I call "thrill-hate crimes." The perpetrators gain very little in a tangible sense from their crimes. Instead, they get bragging rights with their hate-filled friends and an amorphous sense of their own superiority. The more they bash their victims, the better they feel about themselves.

Some teenagers have videotaped their attacks on homeless men. As the camera rolls, you can hear two or three young people laughing uncontrollably as they kick and beat their victim into submission. It is clear that the attackers love the excitement, the "'high" that they get from inflicting pain and suffering. It makes them feel something they have never before felt—a sense of their own superiority, of power and control. They are important people who determine who suffers and who does not suffer, maybe who lives and who dies.

The last time I appeared on an episode of Jerry Springer's show, I was on with three neo-Nazi skinheads from Davenport, Iowa—men in their early twenties who hated Jews, blacks, Latinos, Asians, gays, and almost anybody else who was different from them.[1] Two of the skinheads had come through O'Hare Airport wearing Nazi uniforms; the third was sporting a Charles Manson–like swastika embedded in his forehead. None of them was knowledgeable about Nazi ideology. All of them were marginalized and alienated young guys who probably hated themselves as much as they despised people of color and Jews.

I came on stage during a commercial break about midway through the program and was seated next to the skinhead with the swastika on his head. Not knowing that his microphone was on in the control room, he whispered to his buddy that he wanted to kill me. I guess he didn't like me too much, even though he had only known me for thirty seconds. Was it my religious identity that turned him against me, I wondered?

A producer ran up to me and let me know that my new TV companion was thinking of taking my life and asked what I would like her to do about it. I responded that she should move me away from the three skinheads to the opposite side of the stage. From that point on, there were no wide angle shots encompassing both the three young men and me. Either I was shown alone or they were.

I felt particularly uncomfortable when I was asked, as the three neo-Nazis listened intently, to explain their extreme hatred for minorities. I suggested that they were frustrated in their ambition to be a successful part of mainstream society—they had dead-end jobs, hadn't finished high school, and weren't getting along with their families. But in hate, they found a new surge of superiority and importance. They were now in charge; they were big shots; they decided who would suffer and who would be injured, who was a friend and who was a foe. They felt superior to their enemies. They were asked to be on national television programs and to be interviewed in the newspapers. And that made them feel very good.

I had made a deal with the producers when I accepted their invitation to appear on the program with racist skinheads: the guests would leave first and be driven immediately back to O'Hare Airport for their trip home. Along the way to the airport, however, the three young racists asked their driver to stop so they could see the sights of the big city—Chicago. I guess they were hungry, because they immediately went into a Burger King, where they encountered a multicultural range of humanity among the customers and employees. What started as a shouting match was quickly transformed into a fistfight between the three Nazis and other customers who were less than thrilled with their presence. The police arrived and arrested the three skinheads on a charge of assault. You just don't walk into a fast food restaurant in multicultural, multiracial Chicago wearing Nazi uniforms and not expect an altercation.

Many thrill-hate crimes are committed by young people who, like the three racist skinheads on the Springer show, feel marginalized and alienated. Few of them hold membership in any organized hate group. For the most part, they perpetrate crimes such as intimidation, simple assault, and vandalism. But on occasion, they also commit murder.

Eighteen-year-old Jacob Robida was filled with hatred. In his view, it was all those Jews, blacks, and gays who had made his life miserable, and he would get even. He ultimately planned to commit suicide, but not until he had done something dramatic to publicize the presence of the subhumans and demons in his midst.

On the evening of Thursday, February 2, 2006, Robida left a bloody trail of assault and murder.[2] First, he walked into Puzzles Lounge, a gay bar in his hometown of New Bedford, Massachusetts. Seated on a barstool, he ordered a drink with a fake ID and talked with the bartender on duty, making certain that he was really in a gay bar. Then, he removed a hatchet from his jacket and swung it at a customer's head. But before he could kill anyone, several patrons tackled him to the ground and took the axe. Robida then pulled out a small-caliber handgun, placed it under his chin, and pulled the trigger, intending to take his own life. When the gun jammed, however, he took out a knife and stabbed three customers.

Robida then ran from the bar and jumped into his car parked down the street. He immediately drove back to his mother's apartment for a brief period. It was now 1 a.m., and Robida was bleeding from the head. However, his injury didn't stop him from fleeing the state of Massachusetts to the home of Jennifer Bailey, his thirty-three-year-old girlfriend in Charleston, West Virginia. Together, they drove to Gassville, Arkansas, where they were stopped by sixty-three-year-old state trooper Jim Sell. Robida shot down the officer with a 9-mm. handgun, and then drove on to Norfork, Arkansas, where he had a shootout with local police. Seeing no way to avoid being captured, he shot and killed his girlfriend and then shot himself in the head. Robida died in a hospital in Springfield, Missouri.

I can only imagine how Robida's mother must have felt when she first learned of her son's murder-suicide. Shortly after his deadly assault had been publicized, she got in touch with me to discuss the incident.[3] Probably for therapeutic reasons, Robida's mother was willing, perhaps even eager, to address the motivation for her son's deadly assault. Actually, she was surprised about his choice of gays as his initial target. True, he didn't like gays, but he despised Jews and blacks. The walls of his bedroom were covered with swastikas, Nazi flags, and anti-Semitic writings. He also kept an arsenal of weapons including hatchets, knives, handguns, and a shotgun.

Robida idolized the powerful image of Adolph Hitler, and he is far from the first young killer to do so. Other desperate young people have similarly expressed some adulation for the Nazi dictator, even if their own minority status would have disqualified them for survival under the Nazi doctrine of Aryan superiority. On the Red Lake reservation in Minnesota, for example, a sixteen-year-old Native American high school student killed ten people including himself. As unlikely as it might seem based on his ancestry, the killer had earlier expressed his admiration for Hitler on a neo-Nazi Web site. Similarly, the Columbine killers—Eric Harris and Dylan Klebold—two high school students who shot to death twelve students and a teacher in Littleton, Colorado, idolized the German dictator's image, yet Klebold's mother is Jewish. They chose Hitler's birthday in April as the date on which to commit their deadly rampage. And, twenty-seven-year-old Dion Terres, just before opening fire on customers eating in a Kenosha, . Wisconsin, McDonald's, made a videotape of himself proudly displaying his Nazi flag and praising the wartime strategies of Adolph Hitler.

When I spoke with her, Jacob Robida's mother seemed to me to be a caring and decent person who loved her son and sincerely sought to understand his bizarre and deadly rampage. For one thing, she wondered why he would walk into a gay bar looking for victims. Why not target the minorities and Jews he thoroughly despised? Though this question gave me pause, I suggested that his choice of a target may have been based on convenience or accessibility. Gays were located within his comfort zone; blacks and Jews were not. There were no Jewish or black bars in his hometown, but Puzzles Lounge was well known locally as a hangout for gay men. Moreover, hatemongers usually don't specialize. If they hate blacks, they often hate Jews, Latinos, Asians, and gays. Robida had a Myspace.com Web page that revealed that he was interested in both neo-Nazism and the rap group Insane Clown Posse. According to his mother, he had long suffered from an extreme form of depression that kept him from being effective at work or at home.

Most prejudice is cultural. People learn to hate from an early age from their parents, teachers, friends, coworkers, and the media. They might never translate their bigotry into behavior beyond using stereotypical epithets and telling bigoted jokes. Though many of us would not consider such behavior acceptable, it would likely go no further.

But there is a second kind of prejudice that goes far beyond the norm, and Jacob Robida was apparently afflicted with it.[4] His hatred was pathological rather than just cultural. It was so consuming, so extreme that it ended up possessing him. He seemed to have been totally absorbed in a paranoid delusion that made him become isolated, fearful, dangerous to others, and that ultimately ended his own life.

Mental health researchers now propose medicalizing the most extreme and dysfunctional forms of prejudice by treating pathological hate as an official psychiatric diagnosis. Edward Dunbar, a psychologist at UCLA who has treated dozens of patients for "racial paranoia," suggests that dangerous forms of hate can be reduced by administering an appropriate form of psychotherapy. Alvin Poussant, a psychiatrist at Harvard Medical School, argues that patients who suffer from pathological hate might benefit from antipsychotic medications and other forms of therapy.

Opponents assert that this diagnosis would allow bigots to evade responsibility for their nasty and illegal behavior. They express concern that the hatemongers would be treated as victims rather than perpetrators, even when they are tried for assaulting members of the groups whom they despise.

But it is already the case that a defendant's mental illness can be a mitigating factor in a judge's sentencing decisions. For example, killers may get a lighter sentence, even when not diagnosed as hatemongers, if they can show they were abused as children. It is the plea of "not guilty by reason of insanity"—not a diagnosis of mental illness—that allows defendants to avert criminal responsibility. And only 1 percent of all felony defendants attempt the insanity defense; just one-third of them are declared insane.

More important, the threat from individuals like Robida might be reduced by treating pathological hate as a mental disorder. First, it would help to discredit and stigmatize the prejudices of individuals whose persistent fears of other groups are regarded as a product of disease rather than rational thought. Their stereotyped statements regarding blacks, Muslims, Jews, or gays would be viewed as delusional, entirely lacking in any reality, rather than as normal cases of prejudiced thinking. Also, extremely hateful individuals would no longer be ignored by the mental health profession or treated only for depression but would be more likely to receive the attention that they so sorely need to combat their delusional beliefs.

Even if Robida had received effective treatment in the form of psychotherapy or antipsychotic medication, he would probably still have held bigoted views. But he might not have gone on a rampage.

Many perpetrators of hate crimes have a more practical reason than just to feel some excitement or to get bragging rights with friends. Some of these offenses are, from the viewpoint of the perpetrator, defensive. He sends a message to the victim as well as to every member of the victim's group. You are not welcome in this neighborhood, in this school, on this campus, at this worksite, in this dormitory, or at this party.

As much as I support strong hate crime legislation, there is a limit as to the advisability of giving a lengthy prison sentence to an offender who commits what he considers a defensive hate crime. In 1996, I was asked to serve as an expert witness in a federal cross-burning case.[5] In Salt Lake City, an interracial couple—a white woman and a black man—awoke in the dead of night to see a five-foot wooden cross burning on their front lawn. To the uninitiated, a burning cross may simply constitute an act of vandalism and trespassing, nothing more serious. But to someone who is familiar with the history of slavery and Jim Crow segregation, a cross burned on the front lawn of a black person constitutes a threat to his life. In an almost entirely white neighborhood, a burning cross sends a strong message to any resident who is black, Asian, Latino, or biracial. *You are not welcome here; this is a neighborhood for white people only.*

The perpetrator in this case turned out to be a twenty-two-year-old neighbor, Michael Magleby, who along with a fifteen-year-old companion had spent the evening with friends, listening to "white power" CDs by the group Skrewdriver, whose lyrics included "n-gger get on your boat, n-gger go" and "blacks moved into my neighborhood and my property values went down." The friends also shared racist jokes and used racial slurs. At 1 a.m., after several hours of heavy drinking, they built a cross, carried it to Magleby's jeep, and drove to a gas station, where they filled a beer bottle with gasoline. Arriving at the home of the interracial couple, the two perpetrators removed the cross from the jeep, placed it in the yard, doused it with gasoline, and ignited it.

Magleby and his younger partner then immediately returned to Magleby's house, where they bragged to their friends about the cross burning.

I flew into Salt Lake City and waited for my turn to testify. In the waiting area, I met the black resident who had been victimized by the cross burning as well as one of the federal attorneys assigned to the case. The prosecutor explained that the defendant's attorney had turned down a plea bargain whereby the defendant would have received a two-year sentence in exchange for a guilty plea. I also discovered that the mandatory prison sentence was twelve years, more than most defendants get for committing manslaughter. Given the age of the defendant—twenty-two—I was also concerned that a lengthy prison sentence might only increase his hatred. I spoke with the victim and told him my feelings about what I considered to be an excessive sentence. He had suffered a great deal emotionally because of the cross burning on his lawn, yet he didn't disagree. The two-year sentence offered by the prosecution seemed quite appropriate and reasonable.

A few minutes later, I was told that my testimony would not be needed and I could return to Boston. As much as I support strong hate crime laws, I must admit feeling a bit guilty about having to support what I regarded as an excessively heavy sentence. And I was relieved that I didn't have to testify in this case. Magleby was still convicted of conspiracy to violate the civil rights of the victim and of using fire in the commission of a felony. In 1999, a federal court sentenced the defendant to 144 months of imprisonment and 3 years of supervised release. I very much doubt that a lengthy prison sentence will make him any less bigoted or hate-filled—but, for an extended period of time, it will at least keep him from committing another bigoted act.

Fifty-seven-year-old Joseph Paul Franklin is another candidate for the label of pathological hatemonger. Not unlike Jacob Robida, Franklin was an ardent anti-Semite who also despised blacks and gays. Not unlike Magleby, he was intent on saving the country from what he saw as the devastating influence of outsiders and foreigners.

That is why I was so surprised when Franklin wrote back to me and even offered to speak with me by phone. I am Jewish and should have been regarded by him as the enemy. Yet he seemed rather friendly and cooperative.

Franklin's lawyer had a different way of interpreting Franklin's apparent inconsistencies. He has a generalized hatred for certain groups as a whole—blacks, Jews, gays—but he doesn't necessarily despise all of the people within any of these groups. Actually, this kind of thinking is not unique. There are many individuals who befriend, date, or even marry someone from a group they despise. The reasoning is simple: My friend, my date, my spouse is different. He's not like the others. Franklin is just an extreme example of what happens to many normal people in more moderate terms.[6]

Franklin also appeared to suffer from paranoia; he explained more than once that it was urgent he speak with his attorneys and asked me to let them know that. Franklin was concerned that the prison staff had told his attorneys not to talk with him on the phone or visit. He never told me why.

Franklin said that he was severely abused by his mother throughout his childhood. He also observed his father battering his mother, so that she frequently ended up having to phone the police. As a teenager, he joined the Ku Klux Klan and the American Nazi Party. He even changed his name from James Clayton Vaughn Jr. to Joseph Paul in honor of Joseph Paul Goebbels, Hitler's minister of propaganda. He took the last name of Franklin in memory of Benjamin Franklin. By the time he had reached his late teens, Franklin already believed it to be his mission in life to eliminate from the country all blacks and Jews as well as any whites who liked blacks and Jews. He represents a classic case of an authoritarian personality—someone who grew up powerless, who suffered from the harsh and threatening child-rearing practices of his parents, and who later identified with powerful people in the world, in this case, Hitler and Goebbels. Rather than use his own experience of vulnerability to identify with the suffering of minorities, he instead attempted to eliminate them from the face of the earth. They might remind him too much of his own perceived inadequacies.

Franklin may have taken the lives of as many as twenty people. Despite being nearsighted in one eye and blind in the other, he was an expert marksman. Indeed, he shot and killed most of his victims from a distance of more than one hundred feet. But he would also bomb buildings and commit bank robberies.

According to official reports, Franklin's list of victims is a lengthy one. In 1977, Franklin blew up the home of an Israeli lobbyist in Bethesda, Maryland. Shortly afterward, he blew up a synagogue in Chattanooga, Tennessee. During the same year, he shot and killed an interracial couple in Madison, Wisconsin, and opened fire on a group of worshipers at a synagogue in Richmond Heights, Missouri, killing a forty-two-year-old man.[7]

In 1978, Franklin was suspected of shooting and paralyzing publisher Larry Flynt because his magazine, *Hustler*, had printed photos of an interracial couple having sex. Four months later, he shot to death a black man and injured his white girlfriend in Chattanooga. During the same month, he apparently shot and killed the black manager of a Taco Bell in Doraville, Georgia.

Then, in 1979, Franklin shot to death a fifteen-year-old white prostitute in Dekalb, Georgia, a twenty-seven-year-old black man sitting in a Burger King restaurant in Falls Church, Virginia, and an interracial couple in a shopping mall parking lot in Oklahoma City.

In 1980, Franklin's death toll escalated. He shot to death several more black men in separate incidents in Salt Lake City and Indianapolis and another interracial couple, this time in Johnstown, Pennsylvania. In May, a gunman shot Vernon Jordan, president of the Urban League, in his back as he got out of his car in Fort Wayne, Indiana. Franklin was later acquitted of the shooting for lack of evidence.

Franklin confessed to many of the killings, perhaps falsely in some cases. He is an attention seeker whose aberrant behavior is often motivated by a craving for publicity and celebrity status. He was eager to accept television interviews with well-known correspondents who sought to probe his mind in order to understand his motivation. While the DC Snipers were on the loose in October 2002, Franklin was more than happy to appear on Court TV to give his "expert opinion" about snipers. At one of his murder trials, he fired his attorney and represented himself. Franklin was quite flattered when the judge "puffed him up" by suggesting that he was as competent as any defense attorney that might be assigned to his case. He would talk only to female prosecutors and defense attorneys. He once fired a male lawyer he thought was gay and believed had come on to him. After being found guilty of shooting a Jewish man, he told a reporter that his only regret was that killing a Jew was not legal. And he felt that interracial dating and marriage were morally wrong, justifying his many attacks on interracial couples.

Franklin is now on death row in Missouri. After hearing the verdict and his sentence, he politely thanked the jury for a fair trial and informed them that he would have escaped from prison if he had not been given the death penalty. In 2000, the US Supreme Court denied his appeal, moving him closer to execution.

Only about 5 percent of all hate crimes are committed by the members of organized hate groups.[8] But when a white supremacist group is behind the perpetrators, there is more likelihood that the victim will be assaulted or even murdered. In July 1999, Benjamin Smith, a member of a hate group out of East Peoria, Illinois—known as the Creativity Movement—shot to death a Korean graduate student on the campus of Indiana University; the killer was also a student there. Smith then murdered a black basketball coach at Northwestern University and assaulted six Orthodox Jews. Three weeks later, Buford Furrow, another hatemonger, walked into a Jewish community center in Los Angeles and opened fire on children there. Making his escape, Furrow shot to death a Filipino letter carrier who just happened to be in the wrong place at the wrong time. A photograph later turned up, showing Furrow two years earlier dressed in Nazi uniform at an Aryan Nations conference in Hayden, Idaho.

I recently spoke about hate crimes to the congregation of a conservative synagogue in Framingham, Massachusetts. I emphasized in my presentation the important role that ordinary people play in supporting the perpetrators of bias attacks. *Hate begins in the silence of ordinary people.*

Halfway through my presentation, a thirtyish-looking man, dressed appropriately in a suit and tie, walked into the room and took a seat at an empty table near the front of the room. I suspected that he might be a reporter who was covering my talk for a local newspaper. It turned out that he was the local leader of the National Alliance, a neo-Nazi organization out of West Virginia. Its leader at the time, William Pierce, had been widely thought to have inspired Timothy McVeigh's 1995 massacre of 168 men, women, and children at the Murrah Federal Building in Oklahoma City. Pierce was not directly involved, but his novel about an impending race war in the United States, *The Turner Diaries*, was said to have provided the blueprint for McVeigh's onslaught.

Toward the close of my speech to the Framingham congregation, the National Alliance representative politely raised his hand and asked me why I had not addressed the massacre of millions of Ukrainians by communists in the Soviet Union, many of whom were, he said, Jewish. He continued to hold the floor, accusing Jews of one atrocity after another and belittling those who remember the Nazi Holocaust. I refused to debate him, thinking that I did not want to give him the attention he sought.

After the close of my lecture, a couple of Holocaust survivors in the audience—men in their eighties—attempted to assault him. They were furious. I quickly moved to the public address system and warned members of the congregation that any physical attack on the neo-Nazi would only give him what he wanted—lots of publicity. His tactic was clearly to make his Jewish enemies look as violent as possible, while he passed for a peace-loving advocate of free speech. My plea was to let him go in peace. And they did.

The next day, I received a copy of an e-mail message penned by the same racist who had crashed my presentation. He had sent a summary of his remarks about the Jewish contribution to the murders of

Ukrainians to all members of the National Alliance along with my contact information—phone numbers, address, and so on. He also suggested that his fellow members not attack me. I wasn't worth it, he said. Instead, he urged them to go after the "media Jews." In addition, he placed the same information about me on the National Alliance Web site, so that all members of his organization would see it. I believe that he took great pride in what he had accomplished at the Framingham synagogue. He had disrupted a meeting of Jews and was looking for praise from his bigoted peers.

Fortunately, I never heard from him or his fellow Nazis, but they are still around. Their organization is presently in a state of disarray. Their former leader, William Pierce, recently died of natural causes. Sales of "white power" music through their label, Resistance Records, have declined. Many members, especially the younger skinheads, have become dissatisfied with what they regarded as stagnation within the ranks. A substantial number of members formed a competitive organization known as National Vanguard. A crisis atmosphere developed around the issue of locating credible leadership.

Not every hatemonger makes a career of victimizing people who are different. For most who commit hate homicide, murder is a once-in-a-lifetime activity. On a Saturday evening in 1994, a twenty-four-year-old man, Harold Latour, killed twenty-one-year-old Sam Nang Nhem in a Fall River, Massachusetts, housing project. Nhem was engaged to be married and was the father of a one-month-old boy. He had come to Fall River in 1984, having survived a war in his Cambodian homeland, the brutal violence perpetrated by the Khmer Rouge, and years in a refugee camp in Thailand.

It was a warm evening in August. After attending a family cookout, Nhem and a friend walked a short distance to a trash bin in the project when they happened upon several men fighting. Confronting Nhem, Latour shouted, "I'm gonna knock that gook out." According to court records, he then pushed his victim to the concrete and repeatedly kicked him in the head with his Doc Martens steel-toed boots.

I became involved in the case when the Bristol County prosecuting attorney Robert Goodale decided to go for the charge of hate crime. My assignment was to inform the court as to the history and usage of the term *gook*. I spent an hour or so on the witness stand telling the court about the origin of the racial epithet and stressing that it was used by Americans to describe the enemy during wartime— first, to characterize the Japanese during World War II, then, North Koreans during the Korean conflict, and then, the North Vietnamese during the Vietnam conflict. Finally, the term *gook* has been employed to denigrate any American of Asian descent, whether he has been in this country for generations or a few months, whether he was from China, Japan, Korea, Vietnam, Thailand, or Cambodia.

The successful prosecution of a hate crime depends on locating some evidence of bias on the part of the defendant that would explain his motivation. That evidence may be slurs or epithets used by the offender in interacting with his victim, racist graffiti scrawled by the offender on a wall or driveway, racist propaganda found in the home or car of the offender, an offender's previous record of committing hate crimes, and/or a location where hate crimes are often committed. The use of the term *gook*, then, was important for establishing the defendant's motivation. My testimony suggested that *gook* was the Asian equivalent of the "N" word, another ugly racial epithet.

After deliberating for a period of eight hours, the Bristol Superior Court jurors came back with a conviction. They agreed with the prosecution's argument that Latour's attack was racially motivated—that the victim was killed because he was of Asian descent. As a result, the defendant was given an enhanced sentence on the hate crime charge and was convicted of second-degree murder rather than manslaughter. Latour was given a life sentence with parole eligibility after serving fifteen years.

The Fall River hate crime was spontaneous. The killer never actually planned to take the life of his Cambodian victim; the attack was not premeditated. Latour lost his cool in the heat of an argument and took his anger out on a member of a group he despised. Thus the homicide was still a crime, but it was not first-degree murder.

By contrast, twenty-seven-year-old Kyle Huff, who had moved to

Seattle from his home in Kingfish, Montana, went on a premeditated rampage in March 2006 at an after-rave party. He shot to death six ravers including a fourteen-year-old girl. The case never went to trial because Huff committed suicide, and the residents of Seattle, including the victims' families, were left without any sense of closure.

I was one of four members of an investigative panel mandated by the Seattle police to determine the killer's motivation.[9] Our panel filed its final report on the case in July. We concluded that Huff had carried an arsenal of weapons and ammunition to the crime scene in anticipation of opening fire on his victims. There was no question that the killer had committed a premeditated act of mass murder. He may have been planning his rampage for several days.

We also focused on the role of social isolation in the killer's life. As long as Huff remained at home in Kingfish, he had friends and family to support and encourage him. But Seattle was a different story. He really floundered in both employment and social relations, getting fired from his part-time job delivering pizzas and isolating himself from sources of personal intimacy. He lived with his twin brother but hardly shared his private thoughts and feelings. And there was a limit as to how much he could depend on any one individual, including his brother, to substitute for what was really a tremendous loss of the support he had enjoyed at earlier stages in his life.

Even in Montana he was seen as a reclusive person. In his high school yearbook, students selected the Huff brothers as most lacking in school spirit. But in the small-town environment of Kingfish, he hung out with a number of other marginalized teenagers who encouraged and supported one another. Maybe they weren't accepted widely, but at least they had one another.

In a sense (not a legal sense), Huff's rampage was a hate crime. He targeted the members of a group—not blacks or Jews or Muslims, but ravers—for punishment. ("Ravers" are young people who attend all-night dance parties known as "raves," which are often held in warehouses and saturated with illicit drugs.) He sought to get even, because he blamed ravers for his personal problems, the trouble he had with relationships, and his inability to have any sexual partners over a long period of time. In fact, in a suicide note found weeks after he took his own life, Huff was explicit in his hatred of ravers, arguing that they were destroying the fabric of American society because of their promiscuous sexual behavior. He wrote that they flaunted their sexuality, and he deeply resented it.

I learned an important lesson from the experience of studying Huff's rampage and the reasoning behind it. He was a pitiful character whose bigotry got out of control. He hated ravers, but he also hated himself. Beyond the "normal" hate found in our culture, *there is also a pathological form of hate that can easily destroy the life of a hate-monger as well as the lives of his victims.*

Chapter 7

HIDING DOMESTIC VIOLENCE?

*D*uring the late 1990s, it looked to me as though a serial killer might be operating in suburban towns west of Boston. First, in December 1998, a seventy-five-year-old woman, Irene Kennedy, taking an early morning stroll through a park in the town of Walpole was sexually assaulted, strangled, and stabbed several times both before and after her death. Kennedy and her husband had come to the park together, but then separated briefly—as was their daily habit—to walk different paths and meet back at their car. It was during their separation that the deadly attack took place.

Then, almost nine months later, in August 1999, eighty-two-year-old Richard Reyenger was bludgeoned to death while walking early in the morning through a park in his hometown of Westwood, just a few miles down the road from Walpole. He was found lying unconscious and bloodied along the banks of a local pond where he had fished daily. Reyenger died later that day at Beth Israel Deaconess Medical Center in Boston. The victim's killer has never been found.

More than two months passed, and a fifty-eight-year-old woman from Wellesley, Mabel Greineder, was fatally attacked with a knife and a hammer. It was early in the morning, and she had been walking with her husband, Dr. Dirk Greineder, in a wooded area about a mile from her home. They had separated for a few minutes, and according to Dr. Greineder, he discovered his wife's body upon his return. He immediately phoned 911. The following is a portion of that call:

Dispatcher: Wellesley police. This call is recorded.
Greineder: Help. I'm at the pond. I need some . . . someone attacked my wife.
Dispatcher: Sir, where are you?
Greineder: I am at, at the pond, at Morses Pond, walking . . .
Dispatcher: At Morses Pond?
Greineder: Walking the dog, someone attacked. I left her because she hurt her back.
Dispatcher: OK. You just need to relax because I can't understand what you're saying.
Greineder: Please, please send a car.
Dispatcher: OK. You're at Morses Pond.
Greineder: Pond, yeah.
Dispatcher: Whereabouts at Morses Pond?
Greineder: I'm outside my, my car outside by the gate.
Dispatcher: OK. Hold on one second, OK?
Greineder: Please send someone.
Dispatcher: Wellesley Control to fourteen zero five.
Greineder: Oh my God.
Dispatcher: What, what happened?
Greineder: I, I, I, we were walking the dog. She hurt her back.
Dispatcher: Is she injured?
Greineder: I think she is dead. I'm not sure. I'm a doctor.[1]

The press referred to the three slayings as the "W town murders" for Walpole, Westwood, and Wellesley, and there were enough similarities among the murders to speculate that one killer might possibly have been responsible for all three. I pointed out in a *Boston Globe* article that all of the victims were older individuals—one man and two women. All were walking in a park during the morning hours. And all were killed in an up close and personal style. Statistics show that two-thirds of all homicides are committed with firearms, yet none of the victims had been shot. Murder is disproportionately a big-city crime, but these slayings took place in smaller towns. The victims resided in upper-middle-class communities located in proximity to one another, where murder is extremely rare.[2]

By June 2003, two of the three murders seemed to be solved. The courts had convicted Martin Guy, a forty-four-year-old pizza delivery man who lived nearby, for the premeditated murder of Irene Kennedy. Dental records indicated that a bite mark left by the killer on the victim's body matched that of the defendant. Moreover, DNA found on Kennedy's body matched Guy's DNA from a statewide database. Though he was never charged in the still-unsolved homicide in the nearby community of Westwood, Guy had been responsible for at least one other murder—the stabbing death of a man in nearby Norwood.

Was Guy a serial killer? EMTs who first reached the Westwood victim believed incorrectly that Reyenger had experienced an accidental fall while fishing. According to David Traub, who heads the press bureau in the Norfolk County DA's office, the EMTs, in trying to save the victim's life, virtually trampled on the crime scene, destroying the potential for locating any evidence incriminating any potential suspect. The EMTs were not careless; they did not regard the area as a crime scene and therefore saw no need to preserve it. Guy was apparently in the local area at the time of the Westwood murder, but there was virtually no evidence to implicate him or anyone else. And not every serial killer commits every local crime.

The Wellesley case took a strange turn. The police ended up arresting the victim's husband, a sixty-year-old well-known allergy doctor who had been walking with his wife at the time she was fatally assaulted. The defendant, Dr. Dirk Greineder, certainly did not "look like a killer." Indeed, he was a highly respected member of Boston's medical community, director of clinical allergy at Brigham and Women's Hospital. His three adult children—Britt, twenty-eight, Kristen, thirty, and Colin, twenty-six, steadfastly supported their father in court by proclaiming his innocence. The defense argued that

Mabel Greineder had been slain by an unknown assailant—possibly a serial killer—shortly after the defendant had left her to walk their dog at a nearby pond. But the jury did not agree. It found Dr. Greineder guilty of first-degree murder and sentenced him to a life sentence without parole eligibility. There was no history of violence between Dr. and Mrs. Greineder. He didn't just lose his temper and then impulsively take her life. This was a methodical and premeditated murder.

Though it obviously impressed the jurors enough for a conviction, the evidence against Dr. Greineder was, in some respects, highly ambiguous. There were no eyewitnesses who had actually seen him stab his wife or bludgeon her with a hammer. (Clearly, for the murderer, neither a knife nor a hammer alone would do. She was both stabbed and bludgeoned to death—it was, in essence, overkill.) There was no physical evidence that would have definitively connected the defendant to the commission of the crime, even if it put him at the crime scene and in touch with the victim.

Nevertheless, there was reason to believe in Dr. Greineder's complicity. He was seen by two eyewitnesses who placed him in three different locations close to the crime scene and to a storm drain in which the murder weapons and gloves used by the killer were later discovered.

Moreover, Greineder wasn't exactly the straitlaced and dedicated husband he portrayed himself to be, nor was he a paragon of virtue in his community. It turned out that Dr. Greineder had led a double life that he had hidden from his family and friends. The renowned allergist had clandestinely indulged in escort services, Internet pornography, swinger Web sites, and visits with prostitutes at local hotels. He sent nude photos of himself over the Internet. In court, Greineder confessed that he had visited hookers and had solicited sex from two women he had met online in a chatroom.

Several days before his wife's death, Greineder spent time in a New Jersey hotel room with a hooker. He phoned the same woman to have sex one day after his wife was slain. The jury may have perceived the doctor's behavior as an inappropriate form of grieving. They may have regarded his postmurder liaison as the behavior of a man who, at the very least, didn't care about his dead wife.

During grand jury proceedings, a prostitute testified that the defendant, using the alias Thomas Young, took a room in the Westin Hotel in Boston, where they had sex on two different occasions. He bought her champagne and a bouquet of roses, had sex with her over a ninety-minute period, watched as she showered, and then paid her $450 in exchange for her services. The pseudonym Thomas Young was the name of one of Greineder's college classmates at Yale.

The prosecution argued that Greineder murdered his wife to keep his extramarital sex obsession from going public. It would have torn his family apart and damaged his reputation. Mabel may have learned of his double life and was about to inform others.

Of course, even if the defendant had led a secret sex life outside marriage, that doesn't make him a killer. There is a huge gap between having a tryst with a prostitute and killing your wife. Yet this is the motivation suggested by prosecutor Rick Grundy to explain the defendant's murderous behavior.

The prosecution argued that Greineder had killed Mabel using a two-pound hammer and a four-inch folding knife. He had struck her twice on the head with the hammer and stabbed her numerous times in the neck, chest, and head. Then, he slit his wife's throat with such force that he almost decapitated her. This had to be an excruciating death, and it's hard to believe a husband could do this to his wife. But as years of police records indicate, it does happen.

According to the local police in Wellesley, the murder weapons were discovered in a storm drain near the crime scene. Searching Greineder's home, the police found a pair of brown gloves that were identical to those worn by the killer. Such gloves were sold at a local hardware store where the defendant often shopped. Of course, the same brand of gloves was sold at hardware stores in many locations around the country. But Greineder's DNA matched that found on a brown right-hand work glove in a nearby storm drain along with the hammer and knife used to kill his wife. The left-hand glove also containing the defendant's DNA was discovered a day after the murder in a storm drain some forty feet from the location where he had parked his automobile during his wife's slaying.

Greineder's jacket was stained with Mabel's blood in a pattern of small blood spots that the prosecution argued represented "impact splatter" from the stabbings delivered to the victim's body. Larger blood spots on his jacket indicated that Greineder had lifted his wife's body from behind, held her under her arms, and dragged her off a wooded trail. Prints were left by Greineder's Reebok sneakers next to a pool of his wife's blood and the beginning of a drag mark made by her left foot.

Greineder lost credibility with the jury when he claimed to have searched for a pulse in his dying wife's neck but had absolutely no blood on his hands. Indeed, he had his wife's blood almost everywhere else on his person, but not on the one place you would expect it to be. (Or would you? Ask almost any physician, and you will learn that taking the pulse in a victim's neck does not require using one's hands, only one's fingertips.) Still, the DNA match was strong evidence.

In addition, a store receipt retrieved from the physician's residence indicated that on September 3, 1999, someone from the Greineder household had purchased a box of nails from Diehl's Hardware in the town of Wellesley. Interestingly, store records also showed that the same type of hammer used to kill Mabel was bought only two minutes later at the same cash register by an unidentified customer.

It seems strange that a medical practitioner with knowledge about overdosing on medications would choose to kill his wife in such a brutal and up close manner. Perhaps he believed that a poisoned medication would be too obvious, that a jury was more likely to think of a serial killer rather than a respected doctor when they determined that the victim's throat was slit. After all, her death was the third murder of an older resident in a wooded area in Norfolk County, outside of Boston. The killer might have been a stranger. Perhaps he planted evidence against Greineder in order to frame him.[3]

It is conceivable (but unlikely) that the DNA analysis was profoundly flawed. Forensic labs around the country have struggled to reduce their backlogs of DNA samples to analyze. They have been inundated with requests to examine DNA materials but have not received the funding necessary to do so in a timely and careful fashion. The Massachusetts State police lab is no different. It was recently under fire for mishandling DNA test results in some two dozen cases. Some crimes can no longer be prosecuted because the results of DNA matches were never forthcoming and the statute of limitations has expired. Of course, under such circumstances, a false positive is less probable than a match never being determined. Still, when resources are lacking, mistakes in all directions can occur—no matter how unlikely.

It also seems surprising, at least on the face of it, that such a talented and intelligent man would make so many mistakes in killing his wife. He left his DNA and his blood at the crime scene; he left lots of evidence in the woods. He purchased the weapon at a local store rather than at a distant location where it would never be connected to him.

Of course, murder is usually a once-in-a-lifetime activity. There is no rehearsal; there is no place to go for training. The killer typically is not educated in the art of taking someone's life and getting away with it. He might be a talented physician but not a talented killer. By the time he learns how skilled he is in committing murder, he might be locked away in a cell for the remainder of his life.

Unlike this case, most domestic murder is spontaneous. A verbal exchange between partners escalates out of control. Losing his temper, a man takes a knife from the kitchen drawer and stabs his wife to death. Feeling guilty, he then phones 911 and confesses to the police. There is no trial, there is no challenge to law enforcement because the killer pleads guilty and is given a sentence of manslaughter or second-degree murder. Case closed.

In some instances, the murder comes as no surprise to anyone who had known the couple for any length of time. The husband was extremely possessive. He treated his wife like an object to be manipulated. He was always castigating her. He abused her. There was a separation. When she finally decided to get a divorce, he refused to take no for an answer. A restraining order was issued, but it only made the husband angrier. One evening, after drinking heavily in a local bar, he came back to the home he had shared with his wife and shot her in the head. The police easily located the husband's firearm. They have his fingerprints and DNA. He pleads guilty and gets a life sentence. Case closed. But not in the Greineder case.

Dirk Greineder wrote to me recently and took the opportunity to again proclaim his innocence of all charges.[4] To this day, he takes no responsibility for the murder of his wife, Mabel. He is in the eighth year of a life sentence served in a maximum security prison in Shirley, Massachusetts. In May 2006, he sought a new trial, arguing that the jurors engaged in misconduct, that they were exposed to irrelevant information about his secret life with prostitutes, that DNA testing was conducted improperly, and that he had been deprived of effective legal counsel. Greineder lost this bid for a second trial, but he plans to try again. His grown children continue to support him. They loved their mother, but they do not believe that Greineder is capable of killing her or killing anyone. The jurors disagreed. But juries have been wrong before and will be wrong again. At least the Commonwealth of Massachusetts doesn't execute killers, just in case.

Chapter 8

FIGHTING THE CULTURE OF SILENCE

We learn from an early age not to "tattle." We are taught that it isn't nice, it isn't something that a decent person does. Informing on friends or family members at best is rude and at worst can be associated with the activities of spies and "rats"; in other words, it's not something that trustworthy and honorable people do.

In penitentiaries, an inmate who "snitches" or "rats" on a cellmate falls to the very bottom of the status hierarchy and may be placed in a protective custody unit to protect him from death threats. But snitching can get you killed outside of prison as well. In some high-crime, inner-city neighborhoods, eyewitnesses to a murder—even those who are friends and family of the victim—may refuse to testify in court or to identify the perpetrator because they fear retaliation. In cities across the country, witnesses willing to cooperate with the police have been killed or their families have been targeted before they are able to go to trial. Whereas the national clearance rate for murder is almost 60 percent, the percentage of inner-city homicides that are solved is too often in the single digits.[1]

In Salinas, California, for example, the police assured a young eyewitness to a shooting that he would not be identified. The man who shot an eight-year-old girl would never know his name. Days after speaking with the police, the witness was standing in front of his apartment. When his mother's boyfriend walked outside, a shooter opened fire. The boyfriend was struck by a bullet and taken by med-flight to a hospital, where he eventually recovered. The next day, twenty-year-old gang member Juan Cabrera was arrested and charged with attempted murder. It was his brother, Abraham Cabrera, who had been arrested and identified in the shooting of the eight-year-old girl.

Recently, in South Florida, a Titusville woman, Royneca White, was shot while sitting outside on a warm summer night. More than a dozen bystanders witnessed the shooting, but not one of them has come forward to cooperate with the police. As a result, the investigation continues without an arrest.

In Baltimore, Maryland, seventeen-year-old Rickey Prince witnessed a gang murder and agreed to testify against the killer. But he was kidnapped and fatally shot in the back of the head a few days after a prosecutor mentioned his name in a crowded courtroom.

In some jurisdictions, authorities try to relocate eyewitnesses away from their "danger zone," usually their own neighborhood. In Monterey County, California, the district attorney's office spent $29,000 to move a woman who had witnessed a gang killing from her community to a new area and to help her find a job.

Yet physical safety is only part of the motivation for lack of cooperation with law enforcement or the courts. In many inner-city neighborhoods, there is a long history of antagonism between the police and the African American community. The police are often seen not as allies but as an army of occupation. African Americans' reticence to cooperate often stems from their knowing many black men who have been imprisoned because of false testimony from a police or jailhouse "snitch." There is persuasive evidence that the majority of wrongful death penalty convictions of black men was based on false testimony of individuals who claimed to be eyewitnesses. Since the federal war on drugs began some twenty years ago, the use of informants by police authorities has grown to the point where people who perpetrate crimes know they can escape punishment by giving false testimony. It has been estimated that, in some communities, at least one in twelve young men is serving as a police snitch.

In many high-crime, impoverished neighborhoods, therefore, the message "stop snitching" has gone mainstream and has generalized not just to fabricated testimony, but to any form of cooperation with law enforcement. Platinum-selling rap artist Cam'ron recently told the television program *60 Minutes* that he would never cooperate with the police even if his information could stop a madman from committing mass murder. The words of Cam'ron and other gangsta rappers represent a widespread belief among the young black residents of our major cities. Merchants peddle T-shirts urging black youngsters to keep their mouths closed. They carry the message in bold letters: STOP SNITCHING.[2]

Major cities are not the only areas where young people refuse to cooperate with authorities. In many suburban communities, too, it is simply not considered socially acceptable to inform on a schoolmate. During the late 1990s, when a string of school shootings occurred in suburban areas and small towns around the country, a culture of silence prevented students from informing about a threat overheard in the corridor or about another student carrying a concealed weapon to classes. *It simply was not "cool" to snitch.*

In at least some of the high-profile school shootings, the killer had made threats prior to the violent incident. Kip Kinkel, who went on a rampage at his school in Springfield, Oregon, read aloud from his journal during a class session that he planned to "kill everyone." Similarly, the thirteen-year-old school shooter in Jonesboro, Arkansas, had warned fellow students that he "had some killing to do." Yet no one informed on these kids.

More recently, a number of potential school shootings have been averted, thanks to students who were willing to break the culture of silence and provide information about a threatening schoolmate to a resource officer, a parent, or a teacher, before it was too late. Following the Virginia Tech massacre, for example, a student at Michigan City High School turned in to the principal a threatening note he had found in the school's bathroom. A review of a videotape of the corridor outside the bathroom identified the writer of the note as a fifteen-year-old boy. He was arrested on charges of harassment before he was able to act on his threat.[3]

The culture of silence is nothing new. It was deeply implicated in a nationally prominent murder case that occurred in the spring of 1990 at Winnacunnet High School in Hampton, New Hampshire. A twenty-four-year-old insurance salesman, Gregg Smart, was shot to death with a .38-caliber handgun in the front hall of his condominium in nearby Derry.

It turned out that his wife, Pamela, a twenty-two-year-old former cheerleader and media services director at Winnacunnet High was accused of having orchestrated the attack. According to the official version, Pamela had talked William Flynn, a fifteen-year-old student and her lover, into executing her husband Gregg so that they could be together.

On January 28, 1991, Flynn pled guilty to second-degree murder. His two good friends, Patrick Randall, who was with Flynn at the crime scene, and Vance Lattime Jr., who drove the car to the victim's condo, pled guilty to being accomplices to the murder.

Only Pamela Smart went to trial. In court, she argued her case by reminding the jurors that she alone among the defendants was willing to be tried, indicating that she alone was innocent. In an apparently cold and emotionless manner (that earned her the name "ice princess" in the press), she admitted having an affair with her student but claimed that she had never asked him to murder her husband.[4]

Flynn told the jury a different story: He said that he did not want to kill Gregg Smart but did so because Pamela had threatened to break off their affair. Flynn admitted that he had hated Gregg because of his marriage to Pamela and wanted him out of the way, but he never initiated the murder. That was Pamela's doing. On March 22, 1991, after deliberating for only twelve hours, the jury found Pamela Smart guilty. Judge Douglas Gray sentenced her to life in prison without parole. She is presently incarcerated at Bedford Hills Correctional Facility in New York State.

To this day, Smart continues to proclaim her innocence. She asserts that she never told Flynn to kill her husband; it was entirely his misguided idea. She argues that she should not be serving a life sentence. And there are many people who believe her story.

I spoke with one of Smart's staunchest supporters, Eleanor Pam, a former professor at John Jay College of Criminal Justice who is considered an expert on the subject of women and violence. Dr. Pam is an official spokesperson for Smart and her family. She has a committed belief in Pamela Smart's innocence.[5]

According to Dr. Pam, Smart had no motive to kill her husband, for whom she still grieves. In fact, she had repeatedly attempted to break off her affair with Flynn, but each time she did so, he threatened to kill himself. Shortly after Smart finally did break up with him and then told her husband about the affair, the fifteen-year-old boy, madly in love, decided to kill Gregg.

Eleanor Pam emphasizes that Flynn was the only one of the three boys who even knew Pamela Smart. All instructions to Randall and Lattime came from Flynn, never from his older love interest. She could not possibly have "manipulated" all the participants in her husband's death, because she had absolutely no relationship with any of them, aside from Flynn.

Furthermore, why in the world would Pamela Smart want her husband murdered? There were less risky ways to get rid of him if she wanted him out of her life. She could easily have secured a divorce or even an annulment. They had no children, so there would have been no custody battles. They rented a condominium, so neither Pamela nor Gregg would have lost ownership of their residence. Dr. Pam pointed out to me that "it was 1991, not 1891, so no insurmountable stigma would have attached to the dissolution of the marriage. . . . Smart certainly did not entertain any notion of a long term relationship with this young man. She loved her husband; this was only an affair. Flynn had the motive, not her. He wanted to eliminate his romantic rival so he would have Pamela."

Also according to Eleanor Pam, Smart's characterization as an "ice princess" is completely false. She tried not to express emotion in court out of a sense of her own dignity and on the instructions of her lawyers. In addition, some of her lack of affect was medically induced by large doses of Prozac she had taken to reduce her depression. I would add only that a real sociopath—someone who was able to kill her husband without any feelings of remorse—would probably have given the jury a first-rate performance. She would have played to the hilt the role of the grieving wife, the caring companion, the emotional partner who had strayed but was now entirely remorseful. She would have known how to look more innocent than a genuinely innocent defendant.

In a letter she recently wrote to me from her prison cell at Bedford Hills Correctional Facility, Pamela Smart made it very clear that she continues to take absolutely no legal responsibility for the murder of her husband. She wrote,

Dear Dr. Levin:

I played no role, directly or indirectly, in the murder of my husband. Through these long years, I continue to hold him in my heart and in my thoughts. I miss him terribly. I wonder if the world will ever know that I am innocent . . .

Sincerely,
Pamela Smart[6]

I initially became involved in the Smart case when Vance Lattime's attorney, Marcia Kazarosian, asked me to serve as a consultant. In this capacity, I was able to read the depositions in the case and get to know the social environment that existed at Winnacunnet High School at the time of the homicide. It shocked me to learn that the culture of silence had been alive and well among these high school students. Informing on a peer was so forbidden in the informal student network that even a murder might be tolerated if preventing it meant turning in a schoolmate. I should emphasize that these were middle-class white kids in a suburban community.

According to the testimony of deposed youngsters, for at least several weeks prior to Gregg Smart's murder, dozens of Winnacunnet students were told that the murder would soon occur, but nobody bothered to call 911 or make an anonymous phone call to a teacher or tell a parent. In one incident shortly before Pamela Smart's husband was killed, Vance Lattime begged one of his friends to let him borrow his car for the evening so that he could help kill Gregg Smart. His friend's response? "Sorry, but I have a date tonight. You'd better ask someone else."

At first, I figured that the students who were told beforehand simply did not believe that their schoolmates were serious about committing a murder, so why would they snitch on someone engaging in idle talk or joking about killing someone? Later, I realized that at least some of the students knew but didn't want to say anything that was socially unacceptable, anything that might get them in trouble with their fellow students. Even weeks after Gregg Smart's murder was committed and everybody knew about it, not one student came forward to cooperate with the police and identify the killers.

Winnacunnet was no different in this respect from thousands of other otherwise excellent high schools across the country. Among youngsters generally, informing may be grounds for rejection by their peers. For a teenager who feels insecure about his standing among his schoolmates, being rejected may seem like getting the death penalty. In many places, there continues to be reticence about cooperating with adults, even if it means failing to prevent a violent crime or to prosecute a criminal.

How do we reverse the culture of silence? Any effective effort must focus not on any particular individual but on the community as a whole. In some cities, gang members, clergy, and the police have come together in a spirit of cooperation that has led to a basic change in the thinking of local residents. First, there must be a recognition among local residents that uncooperative eyewitnesses are a threat to everyone in the community. The next victim could be anyone's mother, father, son, or daughter. How will the violence ever stop if residents and the police continue to be at odds? In Boston, for example, black Baptist ministers helped to identify incorrigible youngsters who had engaged in a pattern of serious violence. They also supervised the activities of teenagers in the neighborhoods whose lives could still be saved. Second, gang leaders must be willing to negotiate with one another in good faith before a crisis situation develops between them. In 2006, as the city's murder rate rose, Boston mayor Thomas Menino and Rev. Jeffrey Brown became actively engaged in negotiating a truce between H-Block and Heath Street gang members in the Jamaica Plain section of the city. A cease-fire was maintained between the rival gangs, even after the murder of a former leader of the H-Block gang who had been working to keep the peace.

In high school settings, it is most effective to begin by gaining the cooperation of student leaders who are influential in setting fads, fashions, and trends among their peers. With their assistance, a school can initiate a series of curricular and extracurricular activities—inspirational talks, role-playing exercises, victim-impact statements—designed to motivate a change in the student culture. But there is also the effect of well-publicized countrywide school shootings on those students who are already on the fence. After the Virginia Tech tragedy, the copycat phenomenon ensured that threatening messages and false fire alarms would disrupt the school day for countless students across the country. But in the aftermath of this tragic mass killing, in which twenty-seven students and five faculty members were murdered in cold blood, there was also no way for teenagers to minimize the horrific consequences of students who are angry enough to kill. If there was any denial before Virginia Tech, there is far less today.

Chapter 9

KILLING FOR COMPANY

I never met Jeffrey Dahmer. He was murdered by an inmate at a Wisconsin penitentiary before I got the chance to interview him. I did, however, speak with his stepmother, Shari, to the mothers of several victims, to a good friend of the Dahmer family, and even to the only victim who got away.

Often in serial murder cases, the mother of the criminal is held responsible, at least in the court of public opinion, and this case was no exception. Everybody blamed Shari for her stepson's crimes. Ever since Sigmund Freud founded the field of psychoanalysis, mothers have been blamed for everything that could possibly happen in the course of their children's development and lives. Shari's friends and relatives must have read Freud, because many of them abandoned her, not wanting to be associated with the family of one of the world's most despicable killers.

This does not necessarily mean that they are bad or uncaring people. They simply wish to distance themselves from the unspeakable horror, while seeking an explanation for such a hideous crime. They look first at the family to assign blame, and they often find what they are looking for.

Sarah Croft (a pseudonym) is a case in point. She was a family friend for some fourteen years until the Dahmer tragedy was revealed. And she never blamed Jeffrey's parents, Lionel and Shari, for creating a monster, but she certainly had her complaints about Shari. In April

2007, Sarah told me that she guessed the so-called Cannibal Killer was probably born with the predisposition to take lives. If she faulted the Dahmers for anything at all, it was that they never quite recognized the seriousness of their son's problems, that they didn't make enough of an attempt to stop him.

In 1991, shortly after Jeffrey Dahmer had been arrested, Sarah was clearly struggling with her relationship as a family friend. She told me at the time:

> I feel guilt because in retrospect I saw this coming. Something wonderful happens to someone when they become a mother. Through no fault of her own, Shari Jordan Dahmer was never able to have children, and when she told me she was going to marry Lionel, I said to Shari, here's your chance. You don't have to get pregnant, you don't have to do anything. You have two handsome sons. You have that family now. But she called them her nemesis, and never once—when we were at lunch or out with the girls shopping, all the rest of us talking about our families—never once did she ever mention her children other than to say that she definitely despised David (Jeffrey's younger brother). And she said that Jeff was no Damn good. Shari is the epitomy [sic] of the wicked stepmother.[1]

When I last spoke with her some sixteen years after Dahmer's cannibal murders, Sarah remained steadfast in her criticism of Shari. And it was obvious to me that she felt especially sympathetic toward Jeffrey's younger brother, David, whom she regarded as a real victim. As she said to me, "He gave up his name, family, friends, and even interrupted his education to escape his brother."

Jeffrey's father, Lionel, was a different story. Sarah told me that her children were very fond of him. She described Lionel as looking very much like a stereotypical intellectual: "smallish, very kind, and very funny." Lionel's occupation was in the field of chemistry, but, according to Sarah, his real love was tennis, and he longed for the day when he could retire and become a tennis pro. Once, after she had known Jeffrey's family for many years, Sarah noticed a letter on a table addressed to Dr. Lionel Dahmer. She said, "Lionel, I didn't know you had your PhD. Is your office door labeled, Dr. Lionel Dahmer?" "No," he replied. "Tennis anyone?"

Sarah's criticism stopped short of blaming Shari for her stepson's murderous behavior, but there were many who would have liked to hold her responsible. I am certainly not one of them. Indeed, based on my own conversations with Shari, I am convinced that she was a decent person and a victim of gossip and innuendo. Interestingly enough, Shari Dahmer never even met her stepson until after his eighteenth birthday. How in the world could she have been to blame for how he turned out? Common sense dictates that she wasn't. Yet this fact didn't seem to stop those who looked desperately for clues to explain the inexplicable and who found a satisfactory but unfair answer in the person of Shari Dahmer.

As for Sarah Croft's contention that she could see it coming, Dahmer's hideous crimes were, in all likelihood, unforeseeable. Hindsight is indeed 20/20, and in retrospect, it is all too easy to play psychologist and recognize all of the warning signs. In fact, there are numerous stepmothers who don't get along with the children in their new family. There are numerous children who fail to connect strongly with a parent. There are numerous children who suffer. There may be hundreds of thousands of Americans, perhaps even millions, who have gone through their formative years being abused, sexually molested, abandoned, or adopted under horrific circumstances. But most of these children never kill anyone. Instead, they grow up and out of their painful childhood to become decent human beings.

Still, this kind of pain and suffering takes its toll on our youngsters. Too many develop a deep sense of powerlessness. A few will compensate by inflicting pain and suffering on others. Moreover, a few unfortunate individuals continue to suffer as they make the transition into adulthood and beyond. They drift—from relationship to relationship, from job to job, from city to city, and perhaps from prison to prison. For some reason, they never get over the humiliating experiences of childhood and continue to feel profound alienation when they reach their twenties and thirties. These are the individuals who are at greatest risk of committing serious acts of violence.

Yet there is little evidence to indicate that, while he was growing up, Jeffrey Dahmer's parents provided anything but a caring environment. By most accounts, he seems to have been treated with love and respect. Yet the young Dahmer became more and more withdrawn from the age of four onward. He would spend much of his day simply staring into space. At school, he became the class clown and was regarded as a disruptive influence in the classroom. At the age of eight, Dahmer was sexually molested by an older neighborhood playmate. Two years later, he was already experimenting with dead animals, decapitating mice, mounting the severed head of a dog on a stake, and bleaching chicken bones with acid. On at least one occasion, he may have butchered a neighborhood cat. And he was fast developing a relationship with the remains of animals.

By his teenage years, Dahmer was on his way to becoming a total recluse, rejecting the companionship of boys his own age in favor of continuing his macabre fascination with dead animals. When his parents divorced and he met Shari, Dahmer had already begun to turn for comfort—on a far too frequent basis—to the deadening qualities of the bottle. According to Sarah Croft, Dahmer was known to have taken a thermos bottle of vodka with him to school. Young Jeffrey had been thrown out of every bar in West Akron and had been brought home on numerous occasions in a police car.

In June of the same year, Dahmer, at the age of eighteen, took his first life. He gave a ride to nineteen-year-old Steven Hicks, who was hitchhiking on the outskirts of town. The two men drove to Dahmer's grandmother's house, where they stayed together for a couple of days. When Hicks tried to leave, Jeffrey beat Hicks into submission and then strangled him. Finally, he dismembered his victim's body and buried the remains in a shallow grave behind the house. Nine years would pass before Dahmer killed again, but during this period of time, he was arrested on a number of occasions for drunkenness, disorderly conduct, and indecent exposure.

Moving to Milwaukee at the age of twenty-seven, Dahmer was able to find a job working in a chocolate factory. In the next three years, he murdered sixteen more young men. Typically, he would meet potential victims at a bar and either invite them back to his apartment to drink and view pornographic tapes or offer them money to pose for nude photos. Once he had gotten his victims into his apartment, Dahmer would spike their drinks with a sedative, causing them to become extremely drowsy and disoriented. Dahmer stabbed or strangled each of his victims, had sex with their corpses, and then dismembered each of them with a hacksaw. Before disposing of their remains, Dahmer took Polaroid pictures of his lifeless guests, for the purpose of reliving the good times he had experienced with their dead bodies. He also saved body parts as "trophies," preserving the penises in formaldehyde and boiling the heads to remove the flesh from their skulls. Dahmer placed the hearts and hands in his refrigerator for future use. Eating human flesh gave him an erection.

At the end of May 1991, the thirty-one-year-old cannibal killer came very close to being discovered. A fourteen-year-old Asian boy, whose facility with English was quite limited, had escaped from Dahmer's clutches and managed to inform the police. But when officers arrived at his apartment building, Dahmer was able to convince them that the boy was his nineteen-year-old gay lover rather than a much younger victim. Believing Dahmer's story, the police left the Asian boy in the killer's care. Almost immediately, Dahmer strangled him, had sex with his corpse, and then dismembered his body.

It is ironic that Jeffrey Dahmer, whose crimes are often used as the endpoint on a yardstick for judging the most hideous murders, was no sadist. He never wanted to kill his victims; he tried to minimize their pain and suffering. His motive was to maintain the presence of his guests. *He killed for company.*

At first, Dahmer tried lobotomizing his victims in order to create a collection of sex slaves. He drilled holes in their skulls and poured in acid. But too much damage was done, and they died. Then, Dahmer sedated his victims and strangled them. Dahmer's attempts to reduce his victims' pain would be totally unacceptable to most serial killers, who seek instead to maximize suffering. They enjoy hearing their victims' scream and beg and plead for mercy. It makes them feel so good. After all, they are in charge; they decide who lives and dies; they are responsible for the misery experienced by their inferior victims.

Even Dahmer's cannibalism had an affectionate component. By consuming his victims, he hoped to make them a permanent part of him—literally. There are some cultures that echo this desire by consuming the corpse as part of the funeral ceremony for a loved one. Even more common is the less offensive but similarly motivated practice of consuming an animal on the gravesite of the deceased, or of eating cookies bearing the image of the deceased, or of consuming food and drink while viewing an open casket. From a Freudian point of view, these practices have a cannibalistic aim—they are sublimated, symbolic, and more sophisticated customs than directly consuming human flesh, but they have the same intention—*to maintain the presence of the deceased.*[2]

I interviewed the only victim of Dahmer who lived to tell about it.[3] Tracy Edwards would have been Dahmer's eighteenth victim, but he was both skillful and lucky. Tracy looked like an easy target. The thirty-year-old was slim and diminutive in physical stature, a man who looked like he would be a cinch to overpower. What Dahmer did not realize was that Tracy Edwards was skillful in the martial arts.

According to Edwards, he had seen Dahmer hanging around the neighborhood and at the local mall after work. Finally, Dahmer approached him and his friends, telling them that he had come from Chicago to visit a sick relative. He suggested that Edwards and his buddies join him to buy some beer, get girls, and go down to the lake. One thing led to another, and Dahmer was able to convince Edwards—just as he had convinced his other victims before him—to go up to his second-floor apartment and have a quick beer.

Edwards explained to me the sequence of events. In his apartment, Dahmer offered his guest a beer and then fixed him a rum and Coke, but Edwards felt nauseated by the sedative in his mixed drink and so instead sipped his beer. When Dahmer saw that his visitor had refused to drink the spiked cocktail, he got more physical. He attempted to slip handcuffs on Edwards's wrist, and then took out a long knife from a drawer and held it against his ribs, warning him not to resist and explaining that he only wanted to take some photographs of his guest. Still wielding the knife, Dahmer then guided Edwards to the refrigerator, where he kept his previous victims' hearts, hands, penises, and skulls. Referring to the body parts, Dahmer said, "They are beautiful, aren't they?" He told Edwards that his skull would end up alongside the others and that it would be even more beautiful than the rest. Tracy Edwards was terrified by what he saw.

Then Dahmer walked his reluctant guest into his bedroom. There, Edwards immediately noticed a vat of acid containing decomposing body parts and a wall of photographs featuring Dahmer's victims' bodies in various poses. Some were in handcuffs; others were mutilated. More as a promise than a warning, Dahmer informed Edwards that his photo would soon be on the wall and that it would look even better than the others.

Edwards later recognized some truth in my contention that Dahmer's cannibalism and photo collection were motivated by a desire to maintain the presence of his visitors. When I mentioned this explanation of Dahmer's behavior to him, Tracy replied: "Right. He told me at a certain point that I will never leave him. He will never leave me. I will always be a part of him."

Of course, Tracy didn't notice any affection in the killer's demeanor at the time he was thinking of escape. Dahmer placed the knife against Edwards's groin and demanded that he take off his clothes and pose in the nude. At this point, however, Edwards knew all too well that he was about to be murdered, so he took a chance and hit Dahmer hard with his fist in the head and gave him a swift kick to the face. The cannibal killer was temporarily disarmed and fell to the floor. Edwards may have been small in physical stature, but he was skillful in the martial arts.

Edwards explained to me that there were eight locks on the door to Dahmer's apartment, only one of which opened it. Hitting his captor in the groin one more time allowed Edwards just enough time to run to the front door and turn one of the locks. Purely by luck, he chose the right one on the first attempt. By that time Dahmer had staggered back to his feet. But Edwards had already run from the apartment, through the hallway and down the stairs to the street, where he flagged down a passing police car that happened to be patrolling the neighborhood.

The police officers listened to Edwards's story and took him back to Dahmer's apartment, where they confronted the killer. Dahmer attempted to talk his way out of trouble, explaining that he had had too much to drink and simply had lost his temper with his guest. His story might have worked, if one of the officers hadn't noticed the photos of dismembered bodies hanging on the living room wall and if a second officer hadn't walked into the kitchen and opened the door to the refrigerator. When the three police officers discovered the heads and hearts of several victims displayed in the refrigerator and freezer, Dahmer's story lost credibility. They also spotted a number of hands, testicles, and penises on the kitchen floor. Then, walking into the bedroom, the police opened a file cabinet in which more skulls, genitalia, and an entire skeleton were being stored. Also in the bedroom, they found three human bodies in varying stages of decomposition and a vat of acid containing human remains. Having been discovered, Dahmer finally lost his composure and struggled in vain as the three police officers attempted to subdue him. They took him into custody.

Dahmer's motivation for murder was different from that of the serial killer who seeks to maximize his victim's pain and suffering. Dahmer felt profoundly rejected by living human beings, so he turned for sexual comfort and companionship to the company of corpses. His cannibalism was, at least in part, designed to maintain the presence of his honored guests as they literally became part of him.

Thirteen years earlier, a young man in London, England, went on a killing spree similar to Dahmer's. Henry Nilson would kill his male victims one by one and keep their remains under the floorboards of his single-family home, where the cold slowed down decomposition. Then, at night, he would take a corpse from his makeshift gravesite and prop up his dead guest in a living room chair so they could watch television together. Nilson's motivation was to have companionship. He took the lives of fifteen men whose presence he was able to maintain in a macabre and hideous fashion.

Several years ago, I had lunch with Brian Masters, the English author of a true crime book about Nilson's crimes. I wondered aloud to him whether Dahmer's murders might not have been a copycat version of Nilson's bizarre offenses. But Masters assured me that his book (as well as newspaper reports of Nilson's murders) had had limited distribution in the United States and would, in all likelihood, have been inaccessible to a man like Dahmer.[4]

Still, the similarities between the crimes of Dahmer and Henry Nilson are striking. At the age of thirty-three, Nilson committed his first murder: On New Year's Eve of 1978, he killed fourteen-year-old Stephen Holmes, who had gone drinking with him at a pub and then followed him home for the evening. In order to keep the boy from leaving him, he strangled Holmes with a necktie and drowned him in a bucket of water. He kept the body for seven days, often cradling it in his arms and masturbating in its presence. He then placed the boy's remains under the floorboards in the living room, so as to keep them from decomposing for as long as possible. Finally, he cut up the body and buried it in his garden.

A year passed before Nilson killed again. His second victim was a Canadian tourist who had had a few too many drinks with his host at a local pub and then went back to Nilson's apartment for a few more. Nilson strangled the young man with the cord on his guest's headphones. He cleaned the body and, for a period of two weeks, propped it up in a living room chair where he would watch his favorite programs with it. He then wrapped the corpse in a curtain and placed it under the floorboards. Nilson's pattern was unbroken for a few more years. He strangled and drowned a victim in his sink; he placed the body of another victim in a cabinet underneath his sink, when he ran out of space under the floorboards; he cut up some bodies; he buried body parts in his garden; and he burned some of the remains in a bonfire.

When he moved to a new residence with no floorboards, Nilson continued to kill and then dissect, boil, and cut up the bodies of his victims. He then flushed their remains down the toilet. When the toilet clogged, a drain-clearing company sent a crew to Nilson's apartment, where they discovered the source of the problem: human flesh and bones had blocked the toilet and had caused it to back up into Nilson's bathroom.

In February 1983, Nilson was arrested on his way home from work. After confessing, he was charged and convicted of multiple murder and sentenced to spend the rest of his life in prison.

Not unlike his English counterpart, Dahmer kept the bodies of his victims around for as long as possible. Tracy Edwards, Dahmer's last and only surviving victim, told me about his conversation with Dahmer, in which the killer showed him the body parts he had stored in his refrigerator.

As noted earlier, Dahmer informed Edwards that his heart would find a place alongside the others. I asked whether Dahmer had said this in a threatening tone of voice. Edwards responded that, on the contrary, Dahmer seemed to think of his collection of body parts in a very positive way. *He was doing Edwards and his other victims a favor. They would be immortalized in the realm of his refrigerator.*

Chapter 10

PLANNING AND PLOTTING TO KILL

After reviewing numerous cases of multiple homicide of various kinds, I have come to the conclusion that *planning and premeditation precede many seemingly senseless slayings that may appear to be spontaneous but are not.* Of course, there are many impromptu outpourings of deadly hostility; not all murders are premeditated. In Indianapolis recently, a seventeen-year-old went on a shooting spree, killing one truck driver and injuring another after having an intense and emotional argument with his family over gutting a deer during a hunting trip. The angry young killer had just gone hunting with his relatives and had a rifle in his hands when his level of frustration reached the boiling point. First, he drove to an overpass on Interstate 65 and opened fire on passing motorists. Then, he drove one hundred miles north, stopping on a segment of Interstate 69 to shoot at a couple of trucks. Shortly after "letting off steam," he confessed his crimes to the police and expressed remorse for his deadly outburst. When I was asked by an Associated Press reporter how this case differed from other sniping episodes, I suggested that this was more like the work of a "spree killer," who targets several victims over a short period of time without a cooling-off period. He kills in a state of frenzy. There was really little, if any, planning involved. If the sniper had been more methodical, he probably would have taken out a larger number of victims and would have avoided apprehension for a longer period of time.[1]

By contrast, serial killers typically plan their attacks. They target usually one victim at a time over a period of weeks, months, years, even decades. Because of their methodical approach to murder, serial killers often stay on the loose for long periods. As noted earlier, Ken Bianchi and his cousin Angelo Buono killed ten women and girls in and around Los Angeles. They went out of their way to clean the crime scene and dispose of the bodies. Clifford Olson, who murdered eleven children in British Columbia, took the time to dig graves for all of the bodies of his victims.

Of course, most rules have an exception, and serial murder is no different in this respect. As we have seen, certain serial killers such as Cesar Barone are fairly careless in the manner they approach their crimes. There are even a few cases of serial murder being perpetrated because the killer repeatedly lost his temper.

In Edmonton, Canada, Thomas Svekla, a thirty-eight-year-old former mechanic from Alberta was recently indicted for taking the lives of two local prostitutes. On June 11, 2004, the body of Rachel Quinney, age nineteen, was found dumped in a cluster of trees. On May 8, 2006, the corpse of Theresa Innes, age thirty-six, was discovered stuffed in a hockey bag at a Fort Saskatchewan home. Police allege that she was slain two years earlier, her body moved some 435 miles inside the hockey bag.

On January 2, 2007, the police finally arrested the suspect and charged him with two counts of second-degree murder. Actually, the bodies of eight women have been found in the same area—in the woods east of Edmonton—since 1988, but it is not unusual for the authorities to charge a suspect with only those murders for which they have strong enough evidence for a conviction.[2]

What struck me as unusual—perhaps even unique—was that the defendant had been charged with second-, not first-degree murder. Apparently, the prosecution would argue that the killer never planned his crimes. Instead, he would frequently visit hookers to have sex. For the most part, his visits were pretty much uneventful. Every once in a while, however, when a hooker would say or do something that infuriated him, the suspect would lose his temper and strangle her. Hence, there were two or more unplanned and spontaneous murders. A rare case of serial temper tantrums turned ugly and then deadly!

Unlike spree or serial killers, mass murderers cause the deaths of at least several victims simultaneously in one or two locations. In December 1987, Tilly Guillory of Colorado Springs had the terrible misfortune of hearing that her younger sister Becky and thirteen more family members were massacred by R. Gene Simmons in their Dover, Arkansas, home. Simmons hit his wife Becky with a crowbar across her head and did the same to his twenty-six-year-old son, who was sleeping in an adjoining bedroom. He asphyxiated his granddaughter with a fish stringer while she slept. He killed his four school-aged children one at a time, calling them into his bedroom and then strangling each one with a fishing line. He shot to death his older son and his wife who had come to visit for the Christmas vacation. He then strangled their infant son. He shot to death Sheila, the daughter with whom he had had an incestuous relationship, as well as her husband. He then strangled their two young children, his own grandchildren. Finally, after killing his fourteen family members, Simmons drove seventeen miles into nearby Russellville and killed two more people, a young woman who had spurned his romantic advances and a part-time employee at Taylor Oil, a local company where Simmons had previously worked. Committing the largest family mass murder in American history was apparently not enough for Simmons; he decided to get even with townspeople as well.

I met silver-headed Tilly Guillory on a couple of occasions—once in New York City and another in Boston—while she traveled around the country giving media interviews regarding her brother-in-law's brutal murders.[3] At the time, it was the largest family massacre in American history, and the record has never been broken.

Tilly was able to come to terms with the murders because she came to believe that her sister, nieces, and nephews were in a much better place in death than they had been while under the control of their tyrannical husband and father. Yet Tilly also had to deal with what she sincerely believed to be warning signs that she had ignored. If she had just been more attentive to what was going on in her sister's relationship, could she have prevented the murders? If only she had said to Becky, "Come on, Sis, we'll take care of you. You don't have to stay with Gene."

It is, of course, quite common for the friends and family of murder victims to feel this way after the fact. Just like members of the public, they see all the warning signs in hindsight and suffer pangs of guilt about not having heeded the "red flags" before it was too late.

One of the problems with predicting a hideous crime is that the human mind has trouble accepting the plausibility of such an extraordinary event. Those who loved the victims might have seen the killer's depression or his delusional ideas. They might have noted his abusive and controlling behavior. They might even have speculated about the possibility that Gene and Becky would separate or get a divorce. It is highly unlikely that they would have foreseen R. Gene Simmons killing anyone, let alone all fourteen members of his immediate family.

Finally, there are numerous men who look and act almost exactly like R. Gene Simmons. They are depressed, controlling, isolated, even paranoid, but they never physically hurt anyone. Early in a relationship, a woman might be flattered by a jealous and possessive boyfriend. At this point, she might not recognize that trouble may lie ahead. Later on, it might be a good idea to get this partner the help that he needs in order to lead a normal and productive life. Or, the only viable alternative might be to separate from him on a permanent basis. Though a depressed and controlling man may not make a good husband or father, he won't necessarily turn out to be a killer. After the extraordinary tragedy occurs, of course, this fact is often overlooked by loved ones who feel relentless responsibility and even guilt.

And suppose that Tilly had indeed strongly believed that Gene would become a terrible threat to her sister. Becky's relocating to Colorado might have been the event that angered her husband enough to precipitate his mass murder. Perhaps the body count would have been lower, or maybe he would have killed more people in town. Who knows?

From the beginning, Simmons had control over Becky, and Tilly noticed it. He dominated her; he belittled her, and she put up with it. At first, she loved her domineering spouse because she felt pampered by his attention. Like so many other women who eventually end up in trouble, Becky saw her husband's possessiveness and jealousy as a compliment. *Look how much he adores me. I am flattered.*

As time passed, however, she found her love dying. Simmons became a total control freak, suspiciously examining every move that Becky made and severely restricting his children's freedom of movement. Their small home had no phone. Simmons would not allow it. The children never slept at the homes of their friends. Simmons wouldn't allow it. And then, when Becky discovered that her husband was having an incestuous relationship with their teenage daughter (Sheila), "that is when her love really died."

Simmons came to believe that his family no longer loved him. They were not communicating with him. They didn't defer to him. They no longer gave him the respect that he deserved. At a family meeting nine months before the murders, family members had laughed at him; they refused to take him seriously any longer. He didn't just snap. No, he felt as though they had deeply hurt him, and he would have to make preparations to get rid of them. In the military, deserters may get the death penalty. R. Gene Simmons felt that his family had deserted him.[4]

Mass and serial murder share at least one characteristic aside from their large body counts—both are methodical and planned. Simmons patiently waited for months before executing his family members. He knew that the Christmas vacation would be the next occasion when all of them would come together. His children and grandchildren from Colorado would join their parents, brothers, sisters, and cousins in

Dover, making it possible to eliminate each and every one of them all at once.

Mass killers typically do not suddenly snap. Like Simmons, they plan their attacks over a period of days, weeks, or even months. And they usually select for execution only those individuals they blame for causing their miseries.

For example, Michael McDermott shot to death seven of his fellow employees at Edgewater Technology in Wakefield, Massachusetts, after learning that his wages were to be garnished by the IRS. A day before opening fire on his coworkers, McDermott had left an arsenal of weapons and ammunition under his desk in preparation for his attack. And he didn't aim his weapons at just any coworker, only at those in the human resources and payroll offices—those he blamed for taking his earnings.

Colin Ferguson, a black American originally from the Caribbean, believed that white people were out to get him, so he devised a plan of revenge. Visiting California, he purchased his weapon—a Ruger P-89 9-mm. pistol. He first had to wait in a cheap motel before acquiring his gun, because California had a ten-day waiting period for buying firearms. Then, he waited another nine months for the right time to strike. In December, boarding a Long Island commuter train, Ferguson opened fire on any passenger who was not black, taking the lives of six people, whites and an Asian, before being taken into custody.

Patrick Purdy also waited. He was irate about the changes that had occurred in his hometown of Stockton, California. When he was growing up, the town was mainly white. Now, things were different, and Stockton was dominated by immigrants, by Asians and Latinos, by those he considered outsiders who didn't deserve to be there. From his point of view, the foreigners were taking *his* job and *his* educational opportunities.

Purdy could have acted in haste to get "revenge," but instead he waited patiently, remaining for months in a sleazy motel room, where he rehearsed the logistics of his impending attack with toy soldiers on the toilet and sink of his bathroom. Then, when he was fully prepared,

Purdy drove a couple of miles to the Cleveland Elementary School, where he waited for children to file onto the playground during recess. Once the children were outside, Purdy aimed his AK-47 semi-automatic rifle and opened fire, killing five, all Southeast Asian youngsters.

Most everyday homicides are committed in the heat of the moment. There is little if any premeditation. An individual becomes enraged and loses his temper. If he happens to be carrying a handgun, he is likely to shoot his victim. If he carries a knife, then he uses it to stab the person. Then, as he finally calms down and feels a surge of remorse, the killer phones 911 and waits for the police to arrive and arrest him. He doesn't attempt to escape; he doesn't conceal the body of his victim; he doesn't clean the crime scene.

Multiple homicide is often very different with respect to how the killer approaches and leaves the crime scene. Only spree killers operate in a manner that resembles more mundane forms of murder, with one exception—spree killers are frequently responsible for several deaths.

As we've seen, serial killers may stalk their victims, waiting for the optimal moment to strike. They bring restraints and weapons to the crime scene in preparation for their deadly attack. They take pains to leave a clean crime scene by removing fingerprints, DNA, and other incriminating evidence. They may drive great distances to dump the bodies of their victims in a desolate area. Planning is the hallmark of their modus operandi, both before and after they take a human life.

Mass murderers similarly go to great lengths in planning their assaults. Weeks or months before committing a massacre, they may purchase an appropriate weapon—typically a semiautomatic rifle—and wait for the right moment to open fire, in the hope of maximizing their body count. Unlike serial killers who find pleasure in their victims' pain and seek to avoid apprehension, the mass murderer is frequently on a suicidal rampage. He wants to die, but not until he has gotten sweet revenge against everyone he regards as responsible for his profound miseries. His planning ends when he ends the lives of his victims. At that point, he may place the gun under his chin and pull the trigger, or he may refuse to drop his weapon so as to be killed by police sharpshooters, or he may even beg for the death penalty. There is no need to clean the murder scene or conceal his victims' bodies. He no longer wants to live.

Chapter 11

MOTIVATING MINDLESS MURDER

In 1967, parolee Charles Manson relocated to San Francisco, where the hippie movement was in full bloom. As an accomplished musician who wrote his own music and played guitar, bearded, diminutive Manson easily attracted love children to his cause. They soon became the members of his so-called family, his devoted followers.

Traveling in a black VW bus, the Manson family drove into the desert and eventually wound up on the ranch of George Spahn, where they continued to be a magnet for young people. They were inspired by Manson's message of love and eagerly embraced his drug and sex-saturated lifestyle.

Over a period of time, however, Charles Manson seemed to change his tune. The transition in Manson's thinking was subtle but still striking in its impact. He began to preach to his flock less about love and more about death on a massive scale, about his prophecy of "Helter Skelter" (from a Beatles' tune he distorted in his own mind), an impending race war between blacks and whites that, as he saw it, blacks around the world would eventually win.

The scenario envisioned by Manson was appealing to those young people seeking to do important things with their lives. According to Manson, while the bloodshed of the race war played out, Manson and his family would remain safely tucked away at a desert hideout in

Death Valley. But once the slaughter had ended and the smoke had cleared, they would wrest power away from the victorious blacks, and Manson would rule the world. By the end of the war, Manson envisioned he would have more than one hundred thousand dedicated followers.[1]

In 1969, revolution was in the air. This was the era of the civil rights movement, feminism, antiwar protests, the Black Panthers, the Weather Underground, FALN (Armed Forces of Puerto Rican National Liberation), and the Symbionese Liberation Army. What sounds totally incredible in today's world actually made a bit of sense in the late 1960s. To many of the youthful baby boomers of the day, a race war did not seem like an impossible nightmare.

Yet two years had passed, and Manson's prophecy of Helter Skelter had so far failed to materialize. Blacks had not made their move; revolution may have been in the air, but it was not just around the corner. Therefore, the Manson family would have to take the first step. They would slaughter a group of rich and powerful people, creating a crime scene that would lead law enforcement to believe that black revolutionaries were responsible. These crimes would then precipitate Manson's race war.

To carry out this plan, the Manson family brutally murdered seven innocent people. According to court testimony, Manson never personally harmed any of the victims but gave the orders for several of his "family members" to do his dirty work. And dirty it was. On the evening of August 9, 1969, Manson's loyal followers invaded the Los Angeles home of pregnant Hollywood starlet Sharon Tate. Her husband, film director Roman Polanski, was away in Europe working on a motion picture and was not expected to return until the following day. But Tate was not alone. She was entertaining her friends Abigail Folger and her boyfriend Voytek Frykowski, as well as hair stylist Jay Sebring. By the end of the evening, all of them would lose their lives.

The killers left a grisly and macabre crime scene. When the police arrived, Sharon Tate's bloodied body lay sprawled across the sofa in the living room, where she had been repeatedly stabbed and strangled.

The noose around her neck had been strung over a rafter in the ceiling and tied around the neck of Jay Sebring, whose stabbed and bloodied remains were similarly left in full view. The bodies of Folger and Frykowski lay on the front lawn. And the body of a friend of the caretaker, Steven Parent, was found inside a white Rambler sitting in the driveway. He was not targeted for his wealth or fame but just because he happened to be in the wrong place at the wrong time. In total, the killers had stabbed their five victims more than a hundred times. Three had also been shot. And on their way out, Manson's followers had written the word "PIG" in blood on the front door of Tate's house.

It took less than forty-eight hours for members of the Manson family to strike again, this time at the residence of Leno and Rosemary LaBianca. In the couple's living room, the killers had tied Leno's hands behind his back, stabbed him repeatedly, and strangled him with a lamp cord. They covered the victim's head with a pillowcase, left a carving knife protruding from his abdomen, and carved the word "War" on his body. Rosemary's bloodied body was found in the bedroom, where she had been stabbed repeatedly. Manson's followers then used the blood of their two victims to write "Death to the Pigs" and "Helter Skelter" in various places around the house.

To this day, Manson claims that he was not responsible for the murders. I spoke with him recently from Corcoran State Prison about his justification for saying that he's innocent.[2] He continues to insist that he never gave the orders, that his family consisted of well-educated and intelligent young people who could think for themselves and had free will. They might have thought that Manson was Jesus Christ; they might have wanted to please him. But he never commanded them to kill anyone.

Manson is still crazy like a fox. He enjoys making people squirm. He is highly opinionated, stubborn, intelligent, and preachy. He dominates conversations. He seeks to startle, to shock. For example, he might abruptly end a conversation, "Hands up! The place is surrounded. You're under arrest."

But this does not make him a killer. The court concluded that he had conspired to commit murder, but the court of public opinion continues to deliberate. There may be hundreds, even thousands of people around the country who, to this day, admire and respect Manson. I spoke with one of them, a man in North Carolina, who has followed Manson since the early 1970s. He phoned me recently because Manson had asked him to give me a message. I listened intently while Manson's friend played the convict's tape addressed to me. The message was clear enough: *We must save our environment!*

Whether or not Manson is guilty in legal terms—and it is all but impossible definitively to conclude one way or the other—there is no question at all that Manson was a charismatic figure who was capable of persuading the men and women in his cult as to what had to be done in order to satisfy their objectives. Even if they were not directly commanded by Manson, his followers would have believed they knew what their leader wanted them to accomplish.

Most of the Manson family members were white and middle class. Many were well educated. In high school, one had been voted most likely to succeed. Another had a master's degree in social work. But Manson's followers got something from their leader they never had before—a cause. They really believed that through the race war they had hoped to precipitate they would assume the leadership of the world. Thus, members of the Manson family were as active as Manson himself in committing acts of violence. None of them had been brainwashed. Each was attracted to Manson by the promise of becoming an extremely important, extremely special person who was destined to make a mark on the world.

It is true that many members of the Manson family came from middle-class backgrounds. But it is also important to note that many of his followers were teenagers who had been on their own and were extremely needy. In 1965, Linda Kasabian, the Manson disciple who drove the killers to the crime scene—at the age of only sixteen—had already moved away from her family and started living by herself.

Other family members had been arrested for committing various crimes before they met Manson. In 1966, Susan Atkins was arrested for her role in a gang holdup and for unlawfully carrying a firearm. Clem Grogan was arrested on three separate occasions for possessing drugs, disturbing the peace, and shoplifting. Years after the Manson murders, crimes perpetrated in the name of Manson continued. In 1975, Lynette "Squeaky" Fromme, age twenty-six, begin serving a twenty-year sentence for threatening the life of President Gerald Ford with a gun. And Sandra Good spent ten years in prison as a result of mailing death threats to corporate executives who she claimed were polluting the environment.

The environment has long been a matter of great concern to Charles Manson and his "family." In his conversation with me, I tried to ask him questions about his interviews with Geraldo Rivera and his "crazy dance," which he performs when he gets frustrated with a line of questioning that he finds demeaning. Manson zigs and zags, jumps up and down, and waves his arms back and forth. Instead of answering directly, Manson repeatedly urged that I focus on the "real criminals" in society, those individuals who rob us of our air and water.

In his interviews with Rivera and other talk show hosts, Manson typically begins with a serious discussion of his role in the 1969 murders. Just as he suggested to me, Manson explains that he never ordered the members of his family to torture and kill Sharon Tate or the LaBiancas. Perhaps they had wanted to please him; maybe they had decided that staging the amazingly brutal crimes would achieve what Manson wanted—the hastening of a race war between blacks and whites.

Manson still enjoys playing with other people's minds. When Rivera interviewed Manson and heard the inmate's explanation for his lack of guilt—that he never gave the orders, he would respond, "Charlie, you are an evil monster."[3] Recognizing the futility of continuing to defend himself to a total skeptic, Manson gave up trying to persuade the television personality of his innocence and instead acted as though he was totally out of touch with reality, when in fact he was only looking for a reaction.

Manson's preoccupation with the environment is nothing new, nor is it an issue unfamiliar to his "family." In the early 1970s, Manson coined the acronym "ATWA" (All The Way Alive) in an effort to highlight what he regarded as an urgent need to save the air, trees, water, and animals. He recently directed me to www.atwa.com, a Web site that links to information about various environmental issues. In addition, the Web site www.mansondirect.com contains a recording of Manson in which he discusses, among other things, measures for conserving water and air and a journalist's report from the United Nations suggesting that more than half of the world's largest rivers have been depleted or polluted. Manson's home page also links to several other environmentally informed Web sites.

Yet mansondirect.com is much more than just a Web site for conservationists. Claiming to be the "official site for the Charles Manson truth," it contains an extensive list of his music and conversation CDs and records, his messages to the public, his photographs, and his songs and poetry. The Web site also features a "special announcement" complaining that Manson's mail has been severely disrupted and asking that anyone who can document missing or delayed mail send a letter of complaint to the proper authorities.

Court TV recently interviewed Edward George, a social worker and administrator who counseled Manson on a daily basis, over an eight-year period, while Manson was incarcerated in San Quentin.[4] It was interesting to me that George's observations squared so well with my own and those of so many others who have spoken with Manson. To this day, Manson continues to possess extraordinary charisma. He inspires, he motivates, he converts. He espouses his worldview, talks nonstop about his philosophy. But under certain conditions, Manson can be extremely disruptive, riling up the other inmates with his threats. According to George, Manson can "manipulate the system better than anyone on both sides of the bars."[5] In my conversation with Manson, he informed me that he was the most famous person in history. Thanks to the mass media, he is widely known around the country, if not the world.

Incarcerated for the remainder of his life (he refuses to attend his parole hearings), Manson continues to receive a few regular visitors. He still attracts new followers. In some cases, fellow inmates have become his disciples and send letters to him after they are released. Though he is now in his mid-seventies, young people still write him with expressions of sympathy and love. Some consider him to be a divine prophet. They ask what they can do for him and whether they can join the "family."

Manson always had a gift of gab and still does. He uses his gift to persuade others to do his bidding and is more than capable of impacting his fellow inmates. One of them is Kenny Calihan, a three-time burglar who plea bargained for a lengthy sentence with the possibility of parole. Calihan serves as Manson's friend and appointment secretary, writing back to those who try to reach Manson by mail and arranging interviews, by phone and in person, when the convicted killer gives his approval. The fact that his mail goes through another inmate may support Manson's conviction that his mail, both incoming and outgoing, is not being delivered.

In June 2007, Calihan sent me the following letter, explaining his relationship with Manson and addressing the issue of Manson's guilt or innocence:

> I've known Charles Milles Manson, B33920, since 1992. And due to our conversations from time to time, we have spoken about all sorts of things. But the main thing, Manson has never denied or admitted the murders that took place in 1969, where Sharon Tate and others were killed. Manson has two main girls in his life, and that being Lynette Fromme, also known as "Red," as she is the one who attempted to kill former President Ford. The other girl is Sandra Good, also known as "Blue."
>
> Manson has lost contact with his girls over the years. The daily activity of Manson is that he plays his guitar and uses the phone to call people who he writes faithfully to. As for his health, Manson is seventy-three and does have minor health issues.
>
> Manson is also a very clever and keen person, who is totally aware of his surroundings and listens to what people say before he

speaks. Manson also has a sense of humor at times. But after being in prison/jail since 1969 on these crimes, Manson says he has to keep going for the legacy to live on: but will the legacy live on? That's the question that everyone wonders when he says this, from time to time.

Sincerely,
Kenny Calihan, CSP—Corcoran (California)[6]

In addition to respectful and deferential inmates, there are probably hundreds of Manson fans outside of prison who would gladly follow the dictates of the man they regard as a talented and inspirational leader, if not Jesus Christ. Some are into music and drugs; others share Manson's concern with the environment. Some are probably decent people who sincerely believe Manson's story, true or not, about being a victim of injustice who deserves to be freed. The potential danger is that a few of these fans may be delusional and alienated misfits who revere and admire Manson so much that they would be willing to do almost anything to please him. The psychological forces that propelled members of the Manson family to murder seven people in 1969—the adulation, the hero-worship—continue to be at play today.

Manson has been in and out (mostly in) of reform schools and prisons since he was nine years old. He continues to express disdain for lawyers, judges, the government, Roman Polanski (director and Sharon Tate's husband), the mass media, and John F. Kennedy. He's against pollution and abortions. He talks fondly about Native Americans. He is concerned about preserving the environment, reducing global warming and pollution, protecting animals and trees, and improving our drinking water.

He told my secretary by phone that, after seeing my analysis of a fugitive serial rapist on an episode of *America's Most Wanted*, the inmates now refer to me as Jack the Jackal. I had the distinct impression that this was actually Manson's own personal assessment of me. Even today, Manson maintains his celebrity status. When I spoke with him recently, he again suggested that he was the most famous person who ever lived. He exaggerates, but not by that much.

You have to take what Manson has to say with a large grain of salt—maybe the entire salt shaker. He suggested that he gets along well with the other inmates. When I asked him why, the seventy-three-year-old Manson suggested that it was because he would beat them up otherwise. In fact, Manson gets more mail than any other inmate in the United States, and some of his fellow prisoners would like to do to him what was done to Jeffrey Dahmer—and for the same reason. Manson is a celebrity; they are totally ignored. Like Dahmer, Manson is a household name, a man who continues to attract huge amounts of attention. He may not be the most famous person ever, as he believes, but he is definitely an infamous figure in the annals of true crime. Many other inmates get no mail at all. Manson gets tons of it. Many other inmates never have a visitor or get phone calls. Manson needs a secretary to handle his correspondence. With his fame and importance, Manson only reminds the other prisoners of their isolation.[7]

Chapter 12

TEAMING UP TO KILL

In order to brainwash someone, you almost always have to assume total control over their everyday experiences. As an example, in 1974, nineteen-year-old newspaper heiress Patty Hearst was kidnapped by members of the Symbionese Liberation Army. She was locked in a dark closet for a couple of months, where she was sexually assaulted and tortured. After a period of time, Hearst apparently came to identify with her aggressors, becoming convinced that they had absolute control over her fate. Her fear was eventually overcome by an overwhelming sense of sympathy for the plight of her captors. She came to identify with their cause. She identified with the group to the point of becoming a member and participating in bank robberies and other crimes for pecuniary gain. Hearst was most likely a victim of brainwashing or thought reform, a condition known as the Stockholm syndrome, whereby hostages come to sympathize with their captors' objectives. But she was still found guilty of bank robbery by a jury of her peers and spent time behind bars. In 2001, she was pardoned by President Clinton, but there are still many Americans who believe that Patty Hearst was guilty.[1]

A more recent example of brainwashing can be found in the case of fourteen-year-old Elizabeth Smart. She was snatched from her Salt Lake City family home in the middle of the night and held captive for more than a year. During that time, she had opportunities to escape her kidnappers but never acted on them. Not unlike Patty Hearst, Smart was a prisoner whose very survival depended on the will of her captors. Her life was constantly being threatened, as were the lives of her family members. Smart finally came to believe that her abductors had absolute control over her fate and the fate of her loved ones. So she complied with their demands. But she was molded into a submissive prisoner in awe of her captors, not a full participant.

Some 25 percent of all serial killers operate in teams—lovers, brothers, cousins, or friends who come together for the thrill of committing murder.[2] In many cases, one member of the team is dominant and the other is submissive. One of the partners gives the orders; the other partner complies. One is therefore more persuasive than the other, but this does not usually constitute brainwashing. Even if one partner has credibility with the other, there is an absence of total control in their relationship.

John Allen Muhammad, a former resident of Tacoma, Washington, and one of the so-called DC Snipers, was sentenced by the state of Virginia to die after his fatal shooting of ten people in and around Washington, DC, during a three-week period in October 2002. Collaborating with Lee Malvo, his teenage partner, Muhammad also killed victims in Alabama, Georgia, Louisiana, Arizona, and the state of Washington, singling them out during the course of an armed robbery or as motivated by revenge.

But in the DC area, Malvo and Muhammad apparently selected their victims on a random basis, shooting to death sniper-style a customer walking in a supermarket parking lot in Wheaton, Maryland, a landscaper who was mowing a lawn in Rockville, Maryland, a taxi driver at a gas station in Aspen Hill, Maryland, a housecleaner seated on a park bench in Silver Spring, Maryland, a nanny vacuuming the inside of her minivan at a gas station in Kensington, Maryland, an elderly man crossing the street in Washington, DC, a Vietnam veteran pumping gas at a station in Manassas, Virginia, a father of six at an Exxon station in Fredericksburg, Virginia, an FBI intelligence analyst in a Home Depot parking garage in Falls Church, Virginia, and a bus driver standing on the steps of his vehicle in Aspen Hill, Maryland.

Once the snipers were in custody, some members of the press as well as investigators complained bitterly that too much attention had been given by the media—especially by network and cable TV—to the DC Sniper case. For one thing, the television "profilers" didn't get it exactly right. While Malvo and Muhammad were on the loose, many of the profilers predicted that the killer would turn out to be a white middle-aged man, that the killer was a resident of the Washington, DC, area, or that the killer had a longtime fascination with hunting and shooting, and so on. The real snipers turned out to be black men, one young and the other middle-aged, who had traveled around the country together and weren't from the DC area. They were homeless career criminals who were only interested in hunting humans.

I was one of the television profilers who suggested that the killer was very likely a "white middle-aged male" and was severely criticized for saying so. Such criticism on the part of reporters and TV personalities, as well as members of the public, does not take into account the basis of behavioral profiling.

The FBI's method of behavioral profiling consists of extrapolating from characteristics of a crime scene, forensic evidence, and motivation for the murder to the personality and behavioral characteristics of the killer. Thus, an extremely organized killer—someone who carefully approaches and departs the crime scene without leaving behind lots of evidence—might be seen as a sophisticated and mature individual who is socially competent, lives with a partner, and holds a full-time job.

In the DC Sniper case, television profilers lacked access to behind-the-scenes information about the killers' crime scenes or motivation. For example, the police investigators knew but never made public the fact that Malvo and Muhammad were motivated to extort a large sum of money from the authorities. Knowing this information might have altered the thinking of TV experts, just as it must have changed the thinking of the task force.

The process of profiling employed by television analysts was based mainly on statistics, on playing the odds. Seventy-five percent of all serial killers are white. Thus there are seventy-five out of one hundred chances that the killer in the DC case would be white. More than 95 percent of all serial killers are men. So, there are ninety-five chances in one hundred that the DC Sniper would be a male. These deductions had nothing to do with political correctness or an image of the angry white man, as some commentators suggested. The entire portrait offered by psychologists, psychiatrists, and criminologists who appeared on TV talk shows and newscasts was developed on a statistical basis as well as from personal experiences dealing with similar previous cases. Of course, the DC Sniper case was unique in many important respects and therefore did not conform to many of the patterns familiar to investigators. But the television analysts would not have known that at the time.

Even so, the media experts got more of the facts right than many remember. Many viewers latched onto the incorrect prediction that the killer was white and pretty much ignored any additional information that was proven to be accurate, such as that both of the snipers were men and that one of them was middle-aged, just as many TV analysts had thought. And there was more information from profilers that turned out to be correct. At first, experts speculated that the sniper was a loner. But as the killings progressed without any eyewitness accounts, many of the TV analysts changed their minds. Former FBI agent Robert Ressler, who was a pioneering profiler while he was with the agency's behavioral science unit, was the first to suggest that there were probably two snipers operating as a team (he knew that more than 25 percent of all serial killers operate in tandem). Bo Dietl later said the same. James Alan Fox then speculated that the killers were playing some sort of team sport. Clint Van Zandt brought up the possibility that the killers were down-and-out extortionists who had been unsuccessful in relationships with women. Casey Jordan said that the sniper might be a former member of the military. Pat Brown characterized the sniper as a psychopath who craves a feeling of power. I suggested that he had a failed marriage and that he was getting off on the publicity.[3]

Some commentators had another, even more damning complaint about the television analysts. They speculated that spreading an image of a middle-aged white male killer might have distracted the investigation, delaying the apprehension of the snipers. The reality was quite different. The investigation may have been sidetracked not by the theory of a white killer but by the task force's insistence of a white van being seen leaving one of the crime scenes. White van, not white man! Eyewitness observation is notoriously unreliable, and this fact was sadly reinforced in the DC Sniper case.[4] Indeed, after every sniping episode, any white van in proximity to the crime scene was stopped by authorities. The killers' blue Chevrolet Caprice would have been one of the few vehicles to get through police roadblocks without being stopped and searched.

Could the publicity given the DC Sniper case actually have assisted the police in bringing the killers to justice? We will never know for sure, but we do know that it was a tip from the public that finally led to the apprehension of the snipers. At 3 a.m. on October 24, 2002, someone noticed two men asleep in their blue Chevrolet at a McDonald's rest area off of Route 95 in Frederick, Maryland, and that person phoned 911. When the police arrived, they opened the car's trunk and discovered that Malvo and Muhammad had modified it for the purpose of providing a stable platform from which to shoot at victims. They also found the long-range rifles used by the snipers to murder their victims.

In 2004, a Virginia jury sentenced John Muhammad to be executed, but under the assumption that Malvo was more of an accomplice than an instigator, another jury gave the younger killer a life sentence without parole eligibility. The jury didn't completely buy the defense argument that Malvo was legally insane when he committed the murders, but they may have taken his mental health into consideration when recommending life rather then death.

At seventeen-year-old Lee Malvo's trial for his part in the DC Sniper attacks, two expert witnesses in psychiatry for the defense, Dr. Diane Schetky and Dr. Neil Blumberg, argued that he had been brainwashed by his much older companion, John Muhammad, and was therefore not criminally responsible for the murders. Schetky testified that Malvo did not fully appreciate the seriousness of the consequences of his crimes. Because he failed to distinguish right from wrong, Schetky argued, Malvo met the criterion for being legally insane when he contributed to the multiple homicides in the DC area. She suggested that the defendant had "merged with Mr. Muhammad. He was acting as his proxy. He was like a puppet in his hands." Blumberg similarly told the jury that Malvo had been brainwashed by his accomplice, allowing the teenager to obliterate his feelings and participate in the shootings as Muhammad's "righteous cause."[5]

Dr. Schetky and I were members, along with psychiatrist Gregory Sokolov, of the "Forced to Kill? The 'Brainwashing' Defense and DC Sniper Case" panel at the 2004 annual meeting of the American Academy of Psychiatry and the Law in Scottsdale. Schetky repeated much of the expert testimony she had given earlier in Malvo's defense. During the question-and-answer period following our presentations, some of the attendees—mainly forensic psychiatrists—expressed their displeasure with the brainwashing defense. They believed that the evidence suggested that Malvo should be held accountable for his murderous behavior.

My inclination was to believe that Malvo was legally sane—that he was not a brainwashing victim but a victim of circumstances. Of course, it is indeed likely that John Muhammad was extremely persuasive. He represented a father figure to the much younger Malvo, who sought to have his older partner legally adopt him. It was John Muhammad who had taken Malvo to the United States from his home in Jamaica, where his father had abandoned him and his mother had abused him on a regular basis. The mental health experts who evaluated Malvo in preparation for his trial in Virginia testified that his mother had flogged her son with broomsticks and belts for even the most minor infractions of the rules.

As a panelist, I pointed out that John Muhammad was undoubtedly a significant figure in the life of his partner, yet he hardly had absolute control over Malvo's life. In fact, during their three-week killing spree, Muhammad and Malvo visited with and had extended conversations with several family members. The two men were never thrown totally to their own devices. In addition, Malvo was never tortured by his older companion, nor was he isolated from other sources of influence. It does not appear that Malvo was ever threatened by Muhammad. He wasn't locked in a closet and assaulted; he was never told that his family would be executed if he didn't comply. Obviously, the teenager admired his older companion as a mentor and role model, and he went along with him voluntarily because his relationship had tremendous personal meaning. *That does not constitute brainwashing.* Malvo didn't want to disappoint his important companion, but he was no prisoner. It appears that he may have been just as complicit as Muhammad. During his trial, the seventeen-year-old defendant confessed that he had personally shot at least four more victims, killing two of them.

Killer groupies—women who establish a relationship with death row inmates and other violent prisoners—often believe the deceptive and self-serving explanations of the killers they come to admire and even love. It isn't that the women who fall in love with killers are stupid, because they are usually not. But the men they admire are so manipulative that they can easily convince these women of their own innocence and sincerity. To understand how a decent and intelligent woman could fall for a brutal serial killer, you really have to focus less on her and more on the manipulative and crafty style of the inmate. He may be a true sociopath, but to an adoring fan he looks more like a victim of injustice.

Many inmates are lonely. They don't usually get letters, visits, or phone calls. Some are simply looking for pen pals who will maintain a relationship through correspondence. Of course, they would love to have a visitor or two, but that may not be possible if long distances are involved.

Unlike the typical inmate, high-profile killers become celebrities who get letters and visitors, even marriage proposals. Scott Peterson was convicted of the first-degree murder of his pregnant wife, Laci. He has received a number of marriage proposals. James Ruppert, who killed eleven family members in Hamilton, Ohio, and who is serving a life sentence was visited by an admiring eighteen-year-old woman just days after being incarcerated. Ken Bianchi was married and then divorced while serving his time in Walla Walla.

At one time, I developed a friendship with Kelly Kenniston, a middle-aged woman and aspiring journalist who married Douglas Clark, aka "the Sunset Strip Killer," a death row inmate convicted of murdering six people. According to official reports, Clark had decapitated one of his victims.

Kelly and I had lunch in a restaurant while she was visiting Boston.[6] Later that day, she would appear on the local television program *People Are Talking*, where she hoped to promote Clark's cause. I asked my guest how she got involved with her death row husband. Over clam chowder, Kelly explained to me that she had begun her relationship with Clark by corresponding with the condemned inmate. She wanted to get an interview for a magazine article she intended to write about a serial killer. At that point, she had totally bought the conclusion of the courts that her subject was an evil man. She was certainly not looking for marriage, having already suffered through two divorces.

But one thing led to another—first correspondence by mail and then personal visits, and Kelly ended up establishing a relationship with and marrying the man known as the Sunset Strip Killer. Four months later, she had seen enough. After reviewing the official version of the evidence against the death row inmate, she was sure that Doug Clark was actually a victim of injustice rather than an evil villain.

Kelly became absolutely convinced of her husband's innocence. Despite evidence purporting to implicate Clark in at least some of the murders, despite a jury decision that had put him in line to be executed, she wrote a newsletter and appeared as a guest on radio and television talk shows around the country in order to gain support for getting him off death row.

Actually, there was a complicating factor in the case that left some ambiguities to be resolved. According to the prosecution, Clark had had an accomplice, Carol Bundy, a thirty-six-year-old divorced mother of two young children who many believed had gone along with the murders for the love of her man. According to the prosecution, she was never the instigator, only the follower. Based on this view, Carol was convicted along with Clark but given a lighter sentence. She would be eligible for parole in seven years, whereas Clark was to be executed. Carol never got the opportunity to see outside the prison walls, however, because she died at the age of sixty-one of heart failure while still incarcerated at the Central California Women's Facility in Chowchilla.

The official version of the murders leaves little room for Clark to claim foul play. His first victims, two teenage girls, were kidnapped at Huntington Beach and forced to perform oral sex on Clark. They were then shot in the head, their lifeless bodies dumped in proximity to Sunset Boulevard in Los Angeles. Hence, the designation Sunset Strip Killer was widely used by reporters to refer to Clark. Next, he murdered two prostitutes whose bodies were found by the police, one dumped behind a restaurant in Los Angeles and the other discovered in Studio City. The killer decapitated one of the victims and kept her head in a freezer. At night, Carol Bundy would bring the head to Clark in the shower so that he could play with it. Finally, Clark killed two young hitchhikers whose remains were found on the outskirts of nearby Malibu.

In her plea bargain for a lighter sentence, Carol Bundy confessed that she, too, had committed some hideous crimes both with and without her lover. Before meeting Clark, Bundy had moved into a small apartment in Los Angeles, where she soon became romantically involved with her landlord, the country-and-western singer Jack Murray, a married man with children. Trusting him, she confided in Murray the details of some of the crimes she had committed. When they later grew apart, Bundy feared that Murray would go to the authorities and snitch. One evening, outside a local country-and-western hangout, Little Nashville, where Murray entertained nightly, Bundy lured him to his van with the promise of sex, then repeatedly stabbed him and shot him in the head. She then decapitated Murray and disposed of his head in a deep ravine. It has never been found.

To this day, Doug Clark blames Carol Bundy for everything. He recently told me that she committed the murders along with her real lover and partner, Jack Murray, the boyfriend she confessed to killing.[7] Clark contends that Bundy framed him. According to him, she was a lesbian who actually had no sexual interest in him. She was a manipulative and crafty pathological liar who would say and do anything to save herself. She loved to kill.

According to Doug Clark, Carol Bundy regarded serial killer Ted Bundy (no relation) as a heroic figure. His murders had received tremendous national publicity in 1979, and Carol followed his crimes with great interest. She had, at one time, referred to Ted Bundy as "our modern day Tom Sawyer." Later on, while imprisoned for the Sunset Strip killings, she wrote letters to Ted Bundy, who was on death row at the time.

Clark wrote me from death row that Carol Bundy had patterned the murders after crimes committed by Ted.[8] His objective was to take the lives of fifty to one hundred victims; she planned to kill fifty to one hundred victims. Both Ted and Carol had "kill kits" in their cars that contained the same type of weapons and apparatus, for example, restraints. Both gave the appearance of being decent people. Both engaged in sex with children.

Also according to Clark, Carol had used Ted Bundy's crimes as a model for her copycat murders. For example, on June 1, 1978, Ted killed Brenda Hall; on June 1, 1980, Carol killed seventeen-year-old prostitute Marnette Comer. On June 11, 1978, Ted killed Georgeann Hawkins; on June 11, 1980, Carol killed sixteen-year-old Cynthia Chandler. On July 14, 1978, Ted killed two girls, Janice Ott and Denise Naslund, decapitating Ott; on June 22, 1980, Carol killed two prostitutes, Exxie Wilson and Karen Jones, decapitating Wilson. Not all of the dates match exactly; not all of the killings were imitated perfectly. But there were enough similarities between Ted Bundy's murders and those reportedly committed by Carol Bundy two years later to give some degree of credibility to Doug Clark's contention.

Clark also emphasizes that the court almost always takes the side of female defendants over that of their male partners. When a man and a woman kill together, the man usually gets the harsher sentence. You might see it as discrimination against men based on prejudice against women. The jury believes that the woman went along with the real killer for the love of her man. Clark contends that even in terms of committing acts of extreme violence, the jury will not buy the notion that women can be leaders. In actuality, this is true, but this doesn't let Clark completely off the hook.

In 1958, Charles Starkweather and Caril Fugate crossed the states of Nebraska and Wyoming over an eight-day period, killing nine people. Nineteen-year-old Starkweather was executed; fourteen-year-old Fugate received a parolable sentence. For many years now, she has been a free woman. Did Starkweather deserve his much harsher sentence? He suggested that if he got the electric chair, then Caril should be sitting on his lap.[9]

In the province of Ontario, Canada, Paul Bernardo and Karla Homolka made up another male-female killing team. On Christmas Eve of 1990, on the outskirts of Toronto, Bernardo and Homolka drugged, raped, and murdered Homolka's fifteen-year-old sister, Tammy. Karla soaked a cloth in halothane, an anesthetic used on animals in veterinary clinics, and held it to her sister's nose to put her in an unconscious state. This allowed Paul to sexually assault her. The anesthetic made Tammy so sick that she choked to death on her vomit. Six months later, the couple murdered a fourteen-year-old girl, Leslie Mahaffy, a high school student in Burlington who wanted to become a marine biologist or fashion designer. Leslie's body parts turned up two weeks later in Lake Gibson. Another fourteen-year-old girl, Terri Anderson, was drugged, raped, and killed just five months later. And Kristen French, a fifteen-year-old honors student at Holy Cross secondary school in St. Catherines was kidnapped while walking home from school. Two weeks later, her body was discovered in a nearby ditch.

Bernardo was arrested in February 1993 and convicted two years later of first-degree murder. He received a sentence of life in prison with parole eligibility in twenty-five years. Thinking that Karla was only an accomplice, the court gave her a sentence of twelve years in prison in exchange for her testimony against her husband. Unbeknownst to the court, Bernardo and Homolka had videotaped the torture sessions with their victims, but Bernardo had hidden these tapes in a bathroom ceiling. By the time the incriminating videotapes were discovered, the plea bargain was complete and Karla had been guaranteed an opportunity to regain her freedom after serving just several years behind bars. Viewing the videotapes would surely have altered the decisions of the jurors. Karla is clearly shown on tape participating fully in the sex-slayings of their victims and enjoying every minute of it. But the jury didn't know this. Karla was therefore released from confinement in 2005 and now lives incognito in the city of Montreal, Quebec, where the case received relatively little publicity.

Did Caril Fugate and Karla Homolka get lighter sentences because of their gender? Did Carol Bundy escape death row because she was a woman? Was she actually a manipulative sociopathic killer who had used her street smarts to convince a judge and a jury that she wasn't so guilty after all?

Based on Doug Clark's explanation, Kelly Kenniston was convinced that Carol Bundy was the real killer—that she had committed all of the murders. Kelly claimed to have corresponded with Carol for a year, pretending to be someone else. In this way, she got a good deal of information from Carol, including letters in which the female inmate suggested how much fun it had been to kill and if released how she would take up where she left off—Carol hoped someday to renew her killing spree.[10]

Kelly also rejected the idea that Carol and Doug had been lovers. According to Kelly, Carol admitted to her that she was a lesbian. When asked whether Doug had been circumcised, she couldn't remember and then guessed wrong. Kelly argues that the only indication of Doug and Carol's romantic involvement was found in Carol's self-serving testimony. In addition, Carol was identified as being solely responsible for viciously killing her married lover, Jack Murray,

Clark is still on death row awaiting execution. He recently wrote to me a lengthy letter in which he again presented his detailed and emotional version of the way the crimes were committed. In a word, he continues to blame Carol.[11]

In terms of legal guilt for committing homicide, many people have an all-or-nothing conception. In their view, you are either guilty or innocent. In fact, however, there are degrees of guilt as recognized in criminal law. A husband who can prove that his wife helped to precipitate her demise—her husband shot her to death when he came home unexpectedly and caught her in bed with another man—might get manslaughter and spend a few years behind bars. If his homicide was spontaneous—he lost his temper but never planned to kill his wife—he might be convicted of second-degree murder and receive a lengthy prison sentence. But if a man premeditates his attack—if he buys the murder weapon a few weeks earlier and waits for the optimal moment to strike—he might spend the rest of his life incarcerated or get the death penalty.

Thus, Doug Clark may be guilty but perhaps not guilty enough to deserve his death sentence. We may never know with certainty. Carol is dead. The case is ice cold.

And Doug and Kelly are no longer a couple. He no longer has her as an advocate. In fact, Clark told me recently that Kelly is completely out of his life. "She always assumed she knew better on everything than everyone else," he said. "So good riddance."[12]

Even while confirming her love for Doug, Kenniston made it very clear that her continuing support depended on his innocence. While still married to Doug, she once explained to me, "I am in love with him. But if I found out he was guilty, I'd be gone in a minute. I think that women who marry men they know are guilty are raving lunatics."[13]

Chapter 13

THREATENING TO KILL

It was a sunny Friday morning in July, and the university where I teach was closed. I was spending the day with fellow criminologist James Alan Fox, working at home. We received a phone call from campus security indicating that a man from a small town in West Virginia calling himself Bernie Gates (a pseudonym) had tried to reach us. Gates had read something we had said to a reporter in an Associated Press story about a massacre days earlier, in which James Huberty murdered twenty-one people at a McDonald's restaurant in San Ysidro, California.

We immediately phoned Gates at his West Virginia home. He told us that he was eager to replicate Huberty's rampage, if not his body count. In the AP article, we had suggested that most mass murderers are selective and methodical—in a sense, rational—rather than impulsive and spontaneous, as so many assume. Bernie Gates might have thought that "rational" was somehow a good thing under these circumstances and he wanted to prove to us that he, too, was quite rational.

Gates must have identified with Huberty, who had suffered profound financial difficulties. The West Virginia man told us that he was holed up in the living room of his home with an arsenal of weapons, waiting for the state police to arrive, so that—like Huberty—he could blow away lots of people with an AK-47. Gates's wife and young daughter were asleep in their bedrooms upstairs, totally unaware of his diabolical plan.

We hoped somehow to talk Gates out of his intended rampage. Instead, the obviously distraught man poured out his soul to us, explaining that his local government had stolen valuable real estate belonging to him and that if we didn't get in a car and drive the thousand or so miles to meet with him, he was going to get even with his community by killing as many police officers as possible when they came to his door.

After hanging up with Bernie Gates, we discussed our options and finally settled on phoning the West Virginia state police, hoping to get an enlightened response—one that would end the crisis at hand without provoking bloodshed. In response, the state police were able to locate a neighbor with whom Bernie Gates was friendly who was willing to visit the potential killer and ask him to give himself up to the authorities. Their tactic worked like a charm. Gates's wife and daughter were still asleep in their bedrooms when West Virginia troopers took Gates away in handcuffs. A few days later, he was released and again at home, apparently feeling much better about things. As far as we could determine, Bernie Gates never again threatened to kill anyone.

I learned an important lesson from this aborted act of violence that has stayed with me. *Most people who threaten don't do it; most people who actually take someone's life never bother first to threaten them.* In many cases, the threat is an end in itself. An individual is looking for attention. His anger dissipates. Or, he knows that by writing a threatening letter or making a threatening phone call, he will be taken seriously and might get help or publicity. As for the mass killer, he typically is not interested in warning anybody. His intention is to gain a measure of sweet revenge through the barrel of a gun.

I am not suggesting that authorities ignore threats, especially after the massacres at Columbine and Virginia Tech. Indeed, one of the reasons there have been fewer massacres by students in high schools and middle schools around the country is that the culture of silence has been broken. Too bad we have not been able to break it in major cities where gang members have agreed not to snitch. They consider cooperating with the police a betrayal of their community. But in small towns and suburbs across the country—the very places where school mass murders were concentrated during the closing years of the twentieth century—more students are coming forward to report a threat they overhear in the hallway or a weapon that another student smuggled into the school. And it has made a difference. Mass killings were apparently averted because students in New Bedford and Marshfield, Massachusetts, informed a resource officer after overhearing a threat in the hallway.

So there are some important exceptions to the rule. On occasion, a killer will threaten first and act later. Joseph Harris, a Ridgewood, New Jersey, postal worker, warned his victim, Carol Ott, "I'll get you" in April 1990 and then, true to his word, murdered her in October 1991.[1]

Texas millionaire Allen Blackthorne twice threatened his wife during a nasty custody battle. Ten years later, the mother of six was shot and stabbed to death in her Sarasota, Florida, home by a hit man who was paid by her former husband.[2]

Entrepreneur Alan Mackerley threatened his business rival Frank Black with death after he had been outbid by Black on a lucrative business deal. A year later, Mackerley lured his victim to his Stuart, Florida, home with the promise of a mutually beneficial collaboration but instead fulfilled his former promise by killing Black and dumping his body in the ocean from a speedboat.

A Las Vegas pimp warned two young women, Victoria Magee and Charlotte Combado, that they would end up in shallow graves in the desert if they didn't cooperate in turning tricks for his clients. A few days later, their bodies were discovered in the Henderson desert.[3]

Some killers do leave notes, but not to warn their victims. They might want to explain posthumously the reason for their murder spree. Kyle Huff, the young Seattle man who took the lives of six ravers and then killed himself, left a note for his brother explaining his mass killing. From his viewpoint, the ravers were destroying the country and had to be stopped. R. Gene Simmons, after murdering fourteen family members and two residents of Russellville, Arkansas, left a note in his safe deposit box in which he discussed his feelings about being deserted by his family as well as his other victims. Leonard Lake, one of the two Calaveras County killers who tortured and murdered as many as twenty-five people, committed suicide but left behind a videotaped soliloquy recorded just prior to committing his string of abductions and killings. In it he explains in cold-blooded terms that he was no longer appealing to the women he desired and so intended to take what he wanted by force. Dion Terres also produced a videotape of himself just before going into a McDonald's in Kenosha, Wisconsin, and opening fire on customers and employees. Unlike Lake's sociopathic production, however, Terres seemed to be a psychotic young man who was confused, even out of touch with reality, and filled with hatred for the way he was treated growing up.

I often receive phone calls and letters from individuals who are in trouble or whose loved ones have been killed. Many of these stories have not had happy endings, except possibly from the killers' point of view.

I was recently contacted by Connie Fusillo.[4] In July 1996, the body of her daughter, thirty-two-year-old Marci Martini, was found on the bedroom floor of her Walpole, Massachusetts, condominium. Pills she had taken for chronic depression were strewn around the room. Martini had apparently been dead for several hours when her boyfriend discovered her remains and phoned 911. After speaking with him as well as the medical examiner at the scene, the police first treated Martini's death as resulting from an overdose, probably a suicide, which also explains why the local newspapers barely mentioned the incident. Yet a later autopsy showed that the original report of the cause of death was erroneous. Martini had been strangled—and probably by someone she knew. The amount of medication in Marci's blood was the prescribed dosage. The crime scene had been staged to make it look as though the victim had taken her own life.

Yet a week after the murder had occurred, the DA's office simply could not accept the theory that Marci had committed suicide. An assistant district attorney and a state police detective from the Norfolk County office visited the parents and asked to see Marci's dog Rocky, now living with them. According to Connie Fusillo, the Norfolk County team wanted to determine whether the marks on Marci's throat might have been made by Rocky in an effort to revive her after she overdosed.

More than ten years after the death of her daughter, Connie Fusillo was still looking for answers. There had been no signs of a break-in. Her daughter was in the process of getting a divorce. She also had had an argument with her boyfriend. Marci's body was exhumed in the hope of locating physical evidence under her fingernails. But the fingernails had been cut when the autopsy was performed and then later misplaced. Based on circumstantial evidence, there seemed to be at least a couple of possible suspects, but no arrests were made.

The best I could do for Connie was to contact the district attorney's office. The original DA in the case was no longer in office, and I learned that the current DA, William Keating, had made an attempt to solve the murder but was not able to build a case against anyone. Whatever evidence there might have been at the crime scene was obliterated as a result of the initial but incorrect judgment that Marci Martini had taken her own life. The crime scene had been profoundly compromised.

Sadly, the case gets colder and colder with every passing year. To this day, Martini's killer has never been brought to justice. Only a confession or the testimony of a reliable eyewitness can bring closure.

A week after hearing from Connie Fusillo, I traveled to the small town of Chadron, Nebraska, to speak with the students at Chadron State College. My topic was "hate and violence on campus." Not that Chadron is particularly hate-filled. On the contrary, my impression of the students and faculty was very favorable. A nice campus; a nice small town; decent residents; excellent students. But not unlike many other colleges and universities around the country where diversity is not totally accepted, Chadron State had recently experienced a couple of hate incidents directed against its gay students.

A few months after my visit, the burned body of Chadron State mathematics professor Steven Haataja, age forty-six, was found bound to a tree in a secluded clearing in the hills just south of the school. The police never located a suicide note, nor did they uncover any reason to believe that the victim was thinking about killing himself.[5]

Some speculated that Haataja may have been the victim of a homophobic hate crime, but all evidence indicated that he was heterosexual. Of course, this "detail" has not stopped irrational hatemongers in other locations from committing antigay attacks against straight men who might have seemingly effeminate gestures or expressions. In Bangor, Maine, for example, two teenage boys threw a man off a bridge to his death on the rocks below. They believed their victim to be gay, but he was heterosexual. Not that his being gay would excuse this! Many straight college students have been harassed and bullied based only on a misimpression that they are gay. And even if they were gay, they obviously shouldn't be harassed anyway.

According to local police, there is reason to believe that Professor Haataja may have taken his own life. In January 2006, he had attempted suicide. He had been on antidepressant medications. There was no evidence that anyone else had been at the crime scene when the victim burned to death. On the other hand, according to his good friend, Haataja would never have chosen a painful method for taking his life. And there is also the question of how he was bound at the ankles and torso to a tree. His hands were not bound, so it is possible that the victim tied himself. To this point, the police continue to call Haataja's death "unresolved."

I also received a call from the mother of a twenty-four-year-old missing man, Miguel Oliveras, who was last seen several months before in Portland, Maine, where he had gone to visit a former girl-friend.[6] She worked at a strip club, the Platinum Plus, which is also where Oliveras was last seen when he left with an unidentified man. Was he voluntarily missing? Or was he a homicide victim? His mother, with whom he lived in the Boston area of Hyde Park, told me that he would never stay away so long without contacting her. More-

Serial killer and cannibal Jeffrey L. Dahmer walks into the Milwaukee County Court, Wisconsin, on Tuesday, August 6, 1991, where he was charged with multiple homicide *(AP Photo/Eugene Garcia)*.

In this photo taken October 21, 1985, Richard Ramirez, accused of multiple counts of murder in the "Night Stalker" killings, clenches his fists and pulls on his restraints in a court appearance in Los Angeles. The California Supreme Court upheld his conviction *(AP Photo)*.

Charles Manson, convicted of ordering the Tate-LaBianca murders in 1969, raises an eyebrow during an interview with reporter Geraldo Rivera *(left)* at San Quentin Prison in California, March 17, 1988 *(AP Photo)*.

CHARLES MANSON #B33920
PO BOX 3476 CORCORAN, CA 93212

USA 24

Pike Expedition, November 1806, Rocky Mountains

STATE PRISON CORCORAN

ATWA

Jack levin - Phd
567 holmes hall
Boston, ma

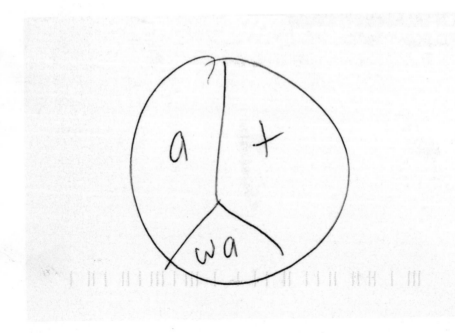

A postcard from Charles Manson writing from Corcoran State Prison depicts his environmental concerns. ATWA is an acronym for Air, Trees, Water, Animals and All The Way Alive. It was first termed by Charles Manson in the early 1970s *(The author's collection)*.

This photo taken in 2007 shows the apartment building at Gainsborough Street where in 1962 the Boston Strangler killed his third victim. To assure that future tenants would not be scared off, the address where the murder occurred was permanently retired (*The author's collection*).

The top photo shows the front of the College of Engineering at the University of Montreal, where in December 1989 Mark Lepine shot to death fourteen female students. A memorial to the slain women *(bottom)* was constructed shortly afterward *(The author's collection)*.

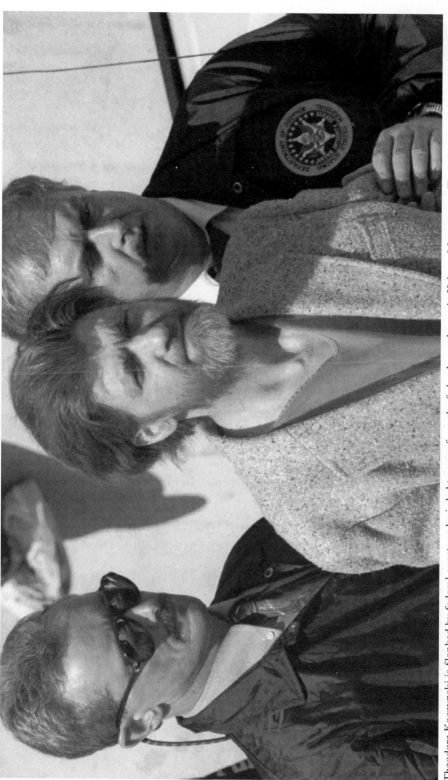

Theodore Kaczynski is flanked by federal agents as he is led to a car from the federal courthouse in Helena, Montana, on Thursday, April 4, 1996 (AP Photo/ John Youngbear).

Orville Lynn Majors *(center)* is escorted into the Vermillion County Courthouse in Newport, Indiana, on January 21, 1998, for his initial pretrial hearing. Majors was later convicted of six murders in connection with deaths at the former Vermillion County Hospital *(AP Photo)*.

In this amateur photo taken at prison in spring 2007, Pamela Smart *(right)* is shown with criminologist Eleanor Pam, who has championed the cause to prove her innocence *(Photo by Eleanor Pam)*.

In December 1987, R. Gene Simmons committed America's largest family massacre in this modest ramshackle house off a dirt road in Dover, Arkansas. Shown on the left side of the photo, Simmons erected a wall of concrete blocks to isolate his family from the outside world (*The author's collection*).

Kenneth A. Bianchi (*left*) sobs in a Whatcom County courtroom on Friday, October 19, 1979, after pleading guilty to the January 11 slaying of two western Washington coeds (*AP Photo*).

Serial killer Cesar Barone seems pensive as he sits through one of his many courtroom appearances in Hillsboro, Oregon (The Oregonian/*Steven Nahl*).

over, she said that he had no vehicle, no baggage, no cell phone, no bank accounts, and very little money. Highly reputable reporter Bob Ward at the local Fox affiliate devoted a news segment to the case of the missing man, but nobody has reported catching sight of Oliveras. Sadly, he may have met with foul play.

I got a phone call from a man in Ohio identifying himself only as a carpenter who expressed his concern about what he called "voodoo cigarette burns" on the faces of notorious killers. He claimed that many sadistic murderers had been branded as children by representatives of a voodoo cult whose beginnings could be traced to the state of Mississippi. Knowing that many brutal killers were tortured as children, an act that caused them to grow up feeling profoundly powerless, I decided to investigate. I phoned outstanding reporter Jerry Mitchell at the *Clarion Ledger* in Jackson, Mississippi. He knew nothing of this claim. I examined a number of photographs of killers—Malvo and Muhammad, school shooter Luke Woodham, serial killer Alton Coleman, but was unable to identify more than a few potential cigarette burns, even in sharp photos. It is possible that many killers are scarred by cigarette burns, but I could not verify it.

During the same week, I heard from Alan Gordon, the police chief in the town of Westborough, a community located west of Boston, where a serial rapist had attacked several women in their homes over the period of a few days. I suggested to Chief Gordon that the so-called Metro-West rapist who attacked in a few communities in proximity to one another would most likely be caught before he struck again. From eyewitness accounts, the police had constructed a composite drawing that they placed on a large billboard overlooking a major highway nearby. The rapist seemed to strike in a frenzied state, not taking pains to disguise his identity or silence his victims. He even left his fingerprints at one of the crime scenes.

Speaking with Chief Gordon, I speculated that the perpetrator probably lived in a nearby town and was familiar with the neighborhoods in which his victims resided. He selected homes on more or less a random basis, entering by an open back door and attacking when he thought the victims were alone. He had probably tried a number of houses but gave up when he had difficulty making entry or when he realized that the victim had company. In one case, he was already in the home of a potential victim before he was aware that her husband was with her. He quickly left the premises, only to invade another residence in the same neighborhood.

A couple of years later, the Metro-West rapist was finally apprehended. He apparently fled the area after recognizing that he would be apprehended if he stayed and began operating again in Moorestown, New Jersey, where he sexually assaulted one woman and broke into the home of another. If the suspect returns to be tried in Massachusetts, he will be charged with aggravated rape, armed burglary, and assault and battery with a dangerous weapon.

I have been asked on a number of occasions to assist someone who is feeling threatened. A few years ago, a janitor who worked in the central administration building of a local school system sent a letter containing a veiled threat to his supervisor. He wrote about feeling mistreated, about being sick and tired of having his grievances ignored. Now, he was looking for revenge.

I suggested that the school system listen carefully to its employee's complaints rather than pass them off as irrational ravings. It turned out that I was correct. School authorities determined that the disgruntled worker had a legitimate grievance that could be easily resolved. That janitor continues to be employed by the same school system where he earlier felt totally alienated. He hasn't harmed a fly—well, maybe a fly, but not his coworkers or his supervisor.

Now, I am not suggesting that threats should be ignored—no, they should always be taken seriously. You never know for certain whether a particular threat might be the exception to the rule. I am arguing in addition, however, that employers should react in a reasonable way to a worker's complaints, preferably long before they develop into murderous intentions.

I recently heard from an attorney in New York City whose ex-employee—a man who had been terminated months earlier under less than amicable circumstances—was sending him drawings in which he threatened to come back to his office on the following Tuesday and kill him. Not knowing where to turn, the attorney phoned to ask me what he should do in order to protect himself. I suggested that he stay away from the office on the Tuesday in question. Instead, the attorney stationed a security guard in the front lobby. Luckily, the ex-worker never showed up. I guess he got enough of a kick just causing his ex-boss some anxiety.

In attempting to assist the attorney, what I really wanted to do was ask why he hadn't gone out of his way to terminate this worker in a humane and decent manner. For many individuals (especially middle-aged men), job loss can be catastrophic. Recognizing this, large companies now exist whose primary business is to specialize in reaching out to a worker as soon as he is fired. They help the terminated employee to write an effective résumé, to use the Internet to locate another position, to rehearse being interviewed, and so on. It's not psychotherapy, but aggressive outplacement counseling that can reduce the potential for crisis. It also happens to be the right thing to do.

Steve Robbins is a friend of mine who owns and manages a deli not far from my house. It is an excellent restaurant, where many local residents go regularly for breakfast or lunch. One of his regular customers is diabetic. Actually, many of them are diabetic, but only this one insisted on testing his blood at the table. On one occasion, his blood spurted everywhere. He left behind a bloody cotton swab, a bloody coffee mug, and a table covered in his blood. Other patrons were sickened. The waitress refused to deal with the situation. The town's board of health advised that "all blood testing is strictly prohibited in any area in which food is prepared, served or eaten."

When he was told by the owner to desist from testing his blood in the dining area, the offending customer refused to comply. He was furious; he was outraged. He argued that he was a victim of discrimination. At this point, concerned about the public health implications, Steve requested that the patron stay away from his restaurant. He was told not to return.

The customer filed a complaint with the state's commission against discrimination, which was summarily dismissed. Then, he filed a second complaint. He began driving past Steve's house, where the owner lives with his twelve-year-old son. He became a general nuisance!

The offending patron had a record going back to 1970 when he was convicted of selling illicit drugs. In 1986, he was placed on probation for an assault and battery conviction. Later in the same year, a restraining order was issued against him when he made a barrage of annoying phone calls to a neighbor. Another restraining order was issued by his ex-wife. In 2004, his intimidating activities escalated to the point where he was following a fellow resident of his town to a couple of Starbucks nearby, driving past his home, and leaving a number of musical voice mail messages on his phone. This time, he was convicted of criminal harassment and again placed on probation.

Fearful of ignoring the harassing behavior of his customer, Steve now feels compelled to go to court in order to get a restraining order. In the meantime, the offending customer is making a career out of intimidation. He is divorced, has no children, lives alone, has no friends, holds no job, has nothing at all to occupy his time. His only pleasure in life comes from causing trouble for other people. At this moment, he has latched onto Steve. I wonder who will be next or how far he will go.

I myself have received threatening letters on several occasions. A number of years ago, I received what I thought was a friendly note from a woman in a small Ohio town who wrote ostensibly for the purpose of complimenting my work as a criminologist. By her tenth letter, however, her tone had turned decidedly ugly. Using one nasty ethnic stereotype after another, she expressed her concerns about all Americans of Polish or Italian descent. They were destroying our country, she claimed, and they were also destroying her life. Her ex-husband was half-Italian, half-Polish and he was a member of the mob, she suggested. She felt a need to seek protection from him.

At first, I considered the possibility that the letter writer from Ohio was a reasonable (if prejudiced) individual who might really have had a run-in with her ex-spouse. But by her twenty-fifth letter, I changed my mind. The woman from Ohio suddenly turned brutally anti-Semitic, accusing me of being in league with her Polish and Italian enemies and threatening to take matters into her own hands—and with her own guns.

And then, her letters stopped coming. I later learned that she had been writing threatening letters to dozens of people, including high-level government officials, one of whom apparently had had her committed as a danger to herself and others. I still have more than one hundred of her bizarre and paranoid letters stored away in a box in my office, just to remind me of the range of responses to my work in criminology.

I once also got a rambling letter from one of Charles Manson's devoted fans, a man in San Francisco who wanted me to know that he did not completely appreciate what I had written about his hero. Actually, my writings about Manson had been entirely descriptive, merely retelling the story of the Manson family murders as they had been reported in the book *Helter Skelter* and in numerous newspaper accounts. But that didn't discourage my detractor one bit. Calling himself Elijah, the Manson follower wrapped his threat around religious passages and spiritual sayings. Because I was about to visit the San Francisco Bay area, I decided to inform the local police there about my threatening mail. They assured me that Elijah was well known to them. He had a list of some fifty people, including the mayor of San Francisco, to whom he had been sending threatening letters. The police assured me that I was actually well down on the list and I therefore need not be concerned about my safety until and unless the mayor were to be assassinated.

I realize now that some people make a career of threatening others. They usually do not follow through. Instead, they get tremendous satisfaction from causing pain and anxiety in the lives of the people they hate. Their threatening messages are in and of themselves a form of revenge.

Chapter 14

VICTIMIZING THE VULNERABLE

I met John Hauser in New York City in 1996, just after the Unabomber had been apprehended.[1] It was early in Hauser's career when Theodore Kaczynski's bomb exploded in his face. In 1985, John Hauser had thoughts of becoming an astronaut. As an air force pilot who had completed almost two years toward his master's degree in engineering at the University of California, Berkeley, John's chances of joining the few Americans who have been jettisoned into space were within the realm of probability. And then, he opened a device on a table, and everything changed.

Before a fairly accurate composite drawing of the killer appeared in newspapers around the country, Kaczynski had personally planted many of his bombs rather than send them through the mail. On May 15, John Hauser was in room 264 of the Cory Hall Computer Science Building, a campus location housing several computer terminals that was frequently used by students and faculty. Kaczynski had left a device on a table in the room in the form of a three-ring binder with blank loose-leaf paper, all affixed to a plastic file box within a wooden frame. It was designed to explode when its lid was opened. It would target the victim's chest and abdomen.

Before Hauser took his place at the table, someone else had apparently moved the device to the side, so that it would naturally be opened more like a book from the side than a briefcase from the front. This change in the positioning of the bomb—rotating it ninety degrees counterclockwise—had the effect of reducing its deadly consequences. Thinking that it was some other student's project, Hauser attempted to lift the binder cover and view its contents. The device immediately exploded, blowing off four of the fingers on Hauser's right hand, temporarily impairing his vision, taking a plug of muscle and nerve out of the inside of his forearm, and leaving him with scars down his arm and across his stomach. Short of causing a death, Kaczynski couldn't have been more pleased with the result he had achieved. He would later gloat about his role in ending the career of someone he felt deserved it—namely, an air force captain.

When I met John Hauser, I was pleasantly surprised by the manner in which he had dealt with his injury. I am sure that the attack left him with very thorny and difficult issues, both physical and psychological, that most individuals never have to face. Still, rather than become embittered and resentful, he seemed at ease with himself and with other people. Apparently, Hauser never gave in to the physical damage that he suffered. Instead, he went on to finish his degree and make a success of his career. It must have been a tremendous burden to realize that there were objectives now out of his reach. He would never be an astronaut, but he persevered. There are some individuals like John Hauser—now a professor of electrical and computer engineering at the University of Colorado—who are able to overcome even the worst sorts of adversity. They are truly survivors.

John Hauser was only one of many Unabomber victims. Over a span of seventeen years, from 1978 through 1995, Kaczynski mailed sixteen bombs, killing three and injuring another twenty-two. The sequence of his bombings was as follows:

DATE: May 1978
LOCATION: Northwestern University
SITUATION: A security guard opens a suspicious-looking package addressed to a professor on campus. The package explodes in his hands.

DATE: May 1979
LOCATION: Northwestern University
SITUATION: A box containing a bomb is left in the university's Technological Institute. A student is injured when he opens the box and the bomb explodes.

DATE: November 1979
LOCATION: American Airlines flight from Chicago to Washington, DC
SITUATION: A bomb airmailed from Chicago explodes aboard American flight 444, forcing an emergency landing at Dulles Airport. Several employees are injured.

DATE: June 1980
LOCATION: Lake Forest, Illinois
SITUATION: A mailed letter bomb explodes, injuring the president of United Airlines when it is delivered to his home in Lake Forest.

DATE: October 1981
LOCATION: University of Utah
SITUATION: A bomb found in a classroom building on campus is disabled by a Salt Lake City bomb squad. No one is hurt.

DATE: May 1982
LOCATION: Vanderbilt University
SITUATION: A box containing a pipe bomb explodes, injuring a secretary on campus.

DATE: July 1982
LOCATION: University of California at Berkeley
SITUATION: A computer science professor is injured when a metal pipe bomb explodes in Cory Hall.

DATE: May 1985
LOCATION: University of California at Berkeley
SITUATION: A bomb explodes in a computer room at Cory Hall, injuring one graduate student (John Hauser).

DATE: June 1985
LOCATION: Boeing Corporation in Auburn, Washington
SITUATION: A package bomb delivered by the post office is safely
    disabled.

DATE: November 1985
LOCATION: Ann Arbor, Michigan
SITUATION: A package bomb mailed to the home of a University of
    Michigan professor explodes, injuring him and his research
    assistant.

DATE: December 1985
LOCATION: Sacramento, California
SITUATION: A bomb planted in front of a computer store explodes,
    killing the owner.

DATE: February 1987
LOCATION: Salt Lake City, Utah
SITUATION: An employee at a computer store is injured when he
    attempts to retrieve a package containing explosives.

DATE: June 1993
LOCATION: Tiburon, California
SITUATION: A package bomb delivered to the home of a University
    of California geneticist injures him when it explodes in his hands.

DATE: June 1993
LOCATION: Yale University
SITUATION: A package bomb sent to the office of a computer science
    professor injures him severely when it explodes in his hands.

DATE: December 1994
LOCATION: North Caldwell, New Jersey
SITUATION: A package bomb mailed to the home of a New York City
    advertising executive kills him when he opens it.

DATE: April 1995
LOCATION: Sacramento, California
SITUATION: A bomb delivered to the office of the California Forestry
   Association kills the association's president when he opens it.[2]

Ted Kaczynski was not always a deranged killer. Nor was he always an angry man. During his late adolescence and early adulthood, Kaczynski seems to have undergone a gradual but profound change in his emotional state. There are some who would argue that he became schizophrenic, and there is considerable evidence that this largely genetic illness often develops when an individual is in his late teens or early twenties.[3]

In the fall of 1958, at the age of sixteen, Kaczynski entered Harvard College as a freshman. At this time, he seemed normal, if not well above average intellectually. After graduation, he earned a master's and PhD in mathematics from the University of Michigan. In the fall of 1967, Kaczynski took a position at the University of California, Berkeley, as an assistant professor of mathematics. He was later promoted to associate professor but resigned his position, relocating to Lincoln, Montana, where he moved into a one-room cabin where he lived for almost twenty-five years. During this period, the Unabomber killed or injured many people.

In July 1995, Ted Kaczynski sent a letter to the *New York Times* indicating that he was ready to stop sending bombs through the mail, but only if the *Times* or the *Washington Post* agreed to publish his anti-industrial, anti-technology 33,000-word manifesto. He wanted Americans to understand why he found it necessary to terrorize and kill—it was a desperate effort to protect the country from a thoroughly dehumanizing society. But was this really his only reason for committing multiple murder?

Also in July of 1995, Kaczynski sent a letter to the *San Francisco Chronicle*, threatening to blow up an airliner at Los Angeles International Airport. Then, a couple of days later, he sent another letter to the *New York Times*, retracting his original threat and indicating that it was only a hoax, just "one last prank."

Why would the Unabomber go through this process of making a threat and then taking it back? I am convinced that one of the prime reasons for his bombing spree can be found not in his philosophical treatise—his manifesto, but elsewhere. The Unabomber loved his celebrity status. Not only did he seek to maximize the terror that he spread across the country, he wanted lots of national publicity.

On April 21, 1995, Timothy McVeigh was arrested in Oklahoma for his role in the bombing of a federal office building and killing 168 men, women, and children. On May 11, McVeigh's partner, Terry Nichols, was also charged for the crime. The events in Oklahoma City received an enormous amount of publicity, as they should have. Indeed, the attention of the nation was focused on McVeigh and Nichols and on the devastation that was caused by these two terrorists. Little attention was paid to the Unabomber, and Kaczynski felt jealous. He felt ignored and wanted some attention too! Hence, the perpetration of a hoax aimed at one of the busiest airports in the United States.

But it was Kaczynski's manifesto printed in the *Washington Post* that finally got him arrested. His brother David recognized certain idiosyncratic aspects of the content and the syntax of the Unabomber's writings and turned him in to the authorities—but not before he had negotiated a deal to save his brother's life.

Arriving early in the morning on April 3, 1996, a SWAT team sur-rounded Kaczynski's Montana cabin, the place where he had lived on his own for some twenty-five years. Kaczynski didn't resist and was arrested without incident. He confessed to having planted the sixteen bombs and is currently serving a life sentence at a federal prison in Florence, Colorado.

Some Americans felt that the Unabomber was a misguided anti-hero who despised what technology was doing to our society and who had decided to send a message of condemnation to the leaders of cor-porate America. I suggested that he was seen by his ardent fans as some kind of a high-tech Robin Hood who wanted to save us from ourselves. I actually said this in an issue of *USA Today*, and got considerable criticism for it.[4] Some who condemned me had not read the entire front-page newspaper article in which I was asked to explain the motivation for a Unabomber fan club, a Ted Kaczynski T-shirt, and a Unabomber legal defense fund. I never expressed my own opinion, which would have been firmly anti-Unabomber. But this detail was lost on those who phoned the president of my university to get me fired. Fortunately, cooler and more rational heads prevailed, and I never suffered for the remarks that I offered to *USA Today* reporters. I did get a kick out of seeing Jay Leno's skit that evening featuring a "high-tech Robin Hood." And I was annoyed with Rush Limbaugh, who claimed that he and his wife had been flying home from Florida when they came across a story in *USA Today* in which I praised Ted Kaczynski. He referred to me as a "liberal Wacko."

I immediately wrote a letter to the editor of *USA Today* in which I suggested that many people, like Rush Limbaugh, had not read the entire story in which I had been cited, but only read a sentence or two taken out of context that could easily be misunderstood. Later that day, Limbaugh apologized. He admitted that he had taken my remarks out of context and that I was not really a liberal wacko after all.

Actually, I never believed that Kaczynski's 30,000-word manifesto published in the *Washington Post* was a political or philosophical treatise. I viewed it instead as an elaborate rationalization for perpetrating murder, written by a deranged individual who loved to kill. He had an IQ so high that he was able to justify his murder spree to the American public at a level not possible for the intellectually less capable serial killer.

Another serial killer who was adept at hiding his tracks murdered at least nine women, over a period of five months in 1988–1989, in the area of New Bedford, Massachusetts. The women had been strangled, most of them with their bras. The victims were marginalized residents—either prostitutes or drug abusers—whose bodies had been dumped in desolate areas off the side of a highway, mostly between Taunton and New Bedford.[5]

To this day, in addition to the nine murder victims, two women from the area continue to be missing, and the case has yet to be solved. The police were never able to find where the murders took place— probably in the car or apartment of the killer. That is where most of the physical evidence would have been located. Murder charges against Kenneth Ponte, a local lawyer and former drug addict who knew several of the victims were dropped because of lack of evidence. Another suspect committed suicide and was never indicted.

The first victim to be discovered, Debra Medeiros of nearby Fall River, was a thirty-year-old woman who was addicted to heroin. On June 23, 1988, almost thirty days after she had disappeared, her mother reported her missing to the local police. Months later, Medeiros's skeletal remains were found dumped in an isolated area alongside Route 140. By April 1989, the ninth body turned up. In August, twenty-five-year-old Sandra Botelho of New Bedford, the mother of two young children, was reported missing. On April 24, a state highway crew, doing a spring cleanup along Route 195 in Marion, discovered her body off the side of the road. Again, the police investigators were left with skeletal remains.

For twenty years, the case of the New Bedford Strangler has grown colder and colder. The original suspects are either dead or have been passed over by a lack of evidence. From the beginning, there were unsubstantiated reports that the local attorney, Kenneth Ponte, who had been indicted in the case, had buried bodies in his front yard. Not believing these reports to be credible, the former local DA never bothered to excavate Ponte's lawn.

In 2007, the new district attorney in Bristol County, Samuel Sutter, made good on his campaign promise to open cold cases including the most famous of all—that of the New Bedford Strangler. The DA looked again at Kenneth Ponte, now fifty-seven, as a suspect and decided to dig up his yard in order to locate any new evidence, including the bodies of the two women who had been missing for over two decades. Neighbors claim they observed the police carrying away bags from the scene, but it appears that nothing of any importance was found in the grounds around Kenneth Ponte's residence.[6]

Certainly the investigators should not have expected to find bodies in Ponte's yard, even if he had been guilty, which likely he was not. Why would a killer who went out of his way to dump the bodies in desolate areas miles away also bury some of his victims so close to home? An organized killer who stays on the loose for decades would hardly make himself so vulnerable. Moreover, the fact that Ponte had previous relationships with several of the victims (he was an attorney for two of them) suggested to me that he was probably not the murderer. Most serial killers—especially those who manage to stay on the loose—target strangers. The last thing they want is to be connected back to the people they victimize.

In addition to those murdered, the children of those victims are also victims. In May 2007, just after the DA in Bristol County had dug up Ponte's lawn, I spoke with the daughter of the New Bedford Strangler's third victim, Debra DeMello—a thirty-five-year-old drug addict who had been last seen by a former boyfriend in New Bedford's Weld Square, an area of the city where prostitutes ply their trade.[7] DeMello's sixteen-year-old daughter was with her mother for the final time when she visited her in the Adult Correctional Institute in Cranston, Rhode Island. Later on, DeMello walked away from a work release program.

The murdered victim's daughter believes that the police felt that "the victims weren't good enough to spend the time solving the cases," because they were prostitutes or drug users, not middle-class college students. She is happy that the new DA has looked again at the murders. In her words, "I want my grandmother to know what happened to her daughter."

Some of the loved ones of murder victims are so angry that they become obsessed with getting revenge. It is understandable when grieving families urge that the killers be executed or when they lobby for strengthening punishments. Some push for the death penalty not to protect others but to exact a measure of what they see as an appropriate form of justice.

There are also many family and friends of victims who don't feel a need to get even and instead decide to honor their fallen loved one by making the world a better place. State Representative Donna Cuomo from the fourteenth Essex district in northeast Massachusetts is a prime example. After fugitive Willy Horton murdered her younger brother Joey Fournier, she established a victim services organization named after the murder victim and helped to place a conflict resolution program in the schools. In the process, she provided the materials for teaching young people anger management, impulse control, and empathy—characteristics that tend to immunize them from becoming perpetrators of violence. At the same time, Cuomo continues to be an advocate for crime victims everywhere.

Matt Zenner had been married to his wife, Teri, for only three months. Although always concerned about her safety on the job, he never really thought that his twenty-six-year-old wife would die at the hands of a crazed killer. A graduate student at the University of Kansas and a social worker for the Johnson County Mental Health Center, Teri was murdered while visiting seventeen-year-old client Andrew Ellmaker in his Overland Park home, which he shared with his mother. Teri had just told Matt that she was making a short visit to be sure that the young man was taking his medication. She would return in no time at all.

Instead, Teri was confronted by her angry client and forced into his bedroom. She begged him to let her go, but as loud music blared in the background, he repeatedly stabbed her in the neck. He then came close to decapitating Zenner as he sliced into her body with a chain saw. During the assault, the young man's mother came home from shopping and tried in vain to plant herself between her son and his victim. Instead of saving Teri, she herself was stabbed in the back multiple times and was lucky to have survived the attack. Meanwhile, Matt Zenner tried getting in touch with his wife by phone. He called his mother, he called her dad, he called anybody and everybody who might know where she was. He sensed that something was terribly wrong.

Zenner's client had been on probation for possessing marijuana.

He was a special-needs student but was academically far behind his age group. The last thing he wanted was to be mainstreamed with much younger classmates. But two days earlier, Ellmaker was forced to start a regular program at a local high school as a sophomore, when he should have been a senior. Rather than attend classes, he spent much of his days hiding in the restroom.

In addition, Ellmaker had long suffered from a chronic mental illness that psychiatrists call schizotypal personality disorder. People with this illness often have trouble connecting with others and usually have few if any intimate relationships. Their social isolation becomes so difficult that, at times, they come to exhibit inappropriate behaviors and develop distorted perceptions of the nature of interpersonal relationships.

Ellmaker had a prior conviction for carrying a concealed weapon, but the mental health center for which Teri Zenner worked would not have been apprised of his record. Instead, social workers were advised to rely on their own judgment as to whether or not a client posed a threat. Their conclusion about Ellmaker: he did not.

Matt Zenner might have become a bitter, withdrawn man in the aftermath of his wife's tragic death, but instead he took a constructive path. For one thing, he established a fully endowed scholarship program in Teri's name for students pursuing a master's degree in social work at the University of Kansas. He made the local mental health board more aware that social workers were at particular risk of being assaulted by their clients and that social workers need training in how to protect themselves. Not unlike security guards, convenience store clerks, cab drivers, and emergency room personnel, many social workers deal with the general public and have little if any say as to who becomes a client and who does not. Unlike most other workers, moreover, there are social workers who deal almost exclusively with individuals who are violence-prone. As a result, the assault rate for social workers is among the highest of any occupational group in our society.

Recognizing the risk in a very personal way, Matt has lobbied for measures to protect social workers in their everyday experiences with potentially violent clients. He told me recently that they should be equipped with pagers that call 911 and have Global Positioning Satellite capabilities.[8] He seeks to ensure that social workers have access to their clients' criminal records.

Matt Zenner also suggested to me that some troubled individuals should probably not be in the community at all, although there are few viable alternatives. During the 1970s and 1980s, many psychiatric hospitals were closed during what was known as the community mental health movement. The humanitarian impulse underlying the movement quickly became perverted by politicians and citizens who were more interested in saving money than lives. It is true that many individuals released from institutions were able to adjust quite well and became productive citizens. But many others were left without adequate supervision to fend for themselves. Some would have done vastly better in an institution. Others posed a threat to the safety of their neighbors but were denied an option that would have been available to them decades earlier. Recognizing the need for a wider range of alternatives for people suffering from severe mental illnesses, Matt Zenner urges that mental health facilities be reopened to provide adequate space for patients who should be hospitalized.

At the national level, Matt has teamed up with Congressman Dennis Moore to work toward the enactment of a federal bill aimed at protecting mental health workers across the country. The legislation would, among other things, fund GPS tracking devices and cell phones and provide necessary training exercises in self-protection and crisis management.

Viewing the crime scene and autopsy photos of his wife's body gave Matt Zenner nightmares for a period of time. But after dealing with Teri's death for more than two and a half years, these graphic photographs also answered a number of unanswered questions, giving Matt a better understanding of the circumstances of his wife's death. A strong and dedicated person, he has been able to move on.

Matt Zenner sat in the courtroom throughout the trial of Teri's murderer. He admitted that some part of him wanted to jump over the railing and get even with the man seated not more than five feet away who was charged with killing his wife. But at the end of the day, it was the jurors and not Matt Zenner who exacted justice, not revenge, by finding Ellmaker guilty of first-degree murder.

I asked Matt Zenner why he decided to take a constructive approach to the healing process in the aftermath of Teri's death. He said, "I could have sat on the couch and cried about it, but I chose to make sure it doesn't happen again."[9]

In a similar example, the death of thirty-three-year-old Peter Goodrich, a victim of the 9/11 attack on America, gave his mother, Sally Goodrich, an opportunity for either living in darkness or causing the light to shine more brightly. The Vermont mother chose sunlight over darkness, altruism over vengeance.[10]

Peter was aboard United flight 175, the second plane to crash into the World Trade Center on September 11, 2001. He was headed for California when his flight was highjacked by the terrorists. Since then, Sally has made a number of trips to Afghanistan, the country that had harbored al Qaeda and the home of the Taliban—training ground for the terrorists who had murdered her son. Who would blame her for despising each and every Afghani she met? Instead, she, her husband Don, and their son Foster created the Peter Goodrich Foundation, raising hundreds of thousands of dollars to build a school for five hundred girls in Logar Province, an hour's drive from Kabul, two schools and an orphanage in Wardak Province, and a well to provide drinking water in Kunar Province. Sally believes that the opportunity to help the children of Afghanistan to get an education restored her own personal faith and gave back meaning to her life and that of her family.

When we think of victims, we might first imagine the suffering of those individuals whose lives were snuffed out by a killer. We might also think of the Tracy Edwards of the world who were caught in a killer's trap and were forced to fight in order to save their lives. Or we might remember the disfiguring pain experienced by John Hauser, whose wounds will never entirely heal. We might want to include the family and friends of the murdered—someone like the young daughter of the third victim of the New Bedford Strangler, Debra DeMello, or like Sally Goodrich, who lost her son to terrorists.

Focusing so much on the horrific pain experienced by the victims' loved ones, we might not give any thought to the family of the killers. Yet these individuals, too, may suffer a great deal. Not only do they lose a son or a daughter or a brother or a sister to death row or the prison system, but they find themselves scorned and stigmatized by those who blame them for bringing up a brutal killer.

I interviewed Frances Piccione, the mother of Hillside Strangler, Ken Bianchi.[11] She had been held responsible by friends, family, and the press for her son's murderous ways. And it was harder for Frances to prove otherwise, because she was Ken's primary caretaker after he had been adopted and while he was growing up in her house.

In response to his attorney's concern about pleading insanity when no evidence of childhood abuse was evident, Bianchi claimed that his mother had held his hand over the burner on the hot kitchen stove as a punishment for his stealing at an early age. The fabrication of this incident was meant to add to the credibility of his insanity defense, but in the end it failed miserably. One of the prosecution psychiatrists was able to demonstrate that Bianchi had feigned insanity (multiple personality) and hypnosis, that he had actually known full well exactly what he was doing at the time of his crimes. He was a classic sociopath, a pathological liar, a manipulative malingerer.

Bianchi manipulated his mother. She was devastated by the discovery of her son's heinous crimes, but she never stopped giving him support. Just after the accusations were made public, Frances relocated from Rochester, New York, where she had lived a respectable middle-class existence, and moved thousands of miles to a trailer park on the West Coast, in proximity to her son's Walla Walla penitentiary address.

When I interviewed her in Boston, she was in tears much of the time, thinking about the way she had been depicted in the court of public opinion. In addition, she was devastated by her son Ken's claim that she had abused him as a child. But as he confessed to me later, he had lied in order to save himself. According to Bianchi, his attorney suggested that his insanity defense would be more likely to succeed if it showed childhood suffering. By the time of my visit to Walla Walla, there was no longer any self-serving motive for Bianchi to maintain that his mother was abusive, so he told the truth.

Like so many other sadistic killers, Ken Bianchi and his older cousin Angelo Buono had maximized the pain and suffering they inflicted on their victims. Many of the girls or young women were taken to Angelo's upholstery shop, where they were tied to a chair and tortured. Some were electrocuted; others were injected with cleaning fluid until they convulsed. Then they were strangled, and their bodies were dumped along the hillsides surrounding Los Angeles.

None of the Hillside Strangler victims were responsible for their fate. Short of taking commonsense precautions, there isn't much that a potential victim can do to protect against a killer who is intent on taking lives. He may lure his victims on the pretext of wanting to be helpful or asking for help. He may strike during broad daylight while his potential victims are jogging on the sidewalk. He may wear the uniform of a police officer or a paramedic. He may invade an apartment or a house in the dead of night. He may answer classified ads and then abduct the individuals selling their furniture.

People simply minding their own business may end up as victims. On occasion, a deranged individual opens fire in a shopping mall, shooting indiscriminately at anyone he encounters. He doesn't have anything against the particular individuals he targets—indeed, he may not even know them. But he has suffered over many years and seeks revenge against humankind. His victims just happen to be in the wrong place at the wrong time.

In October 1985, a customer opened fire with a .22-caliber semi-automatic rifle at a shopping mall in Springfield, Pennsylvania. In this exceptional case, she—the killer was twenty-five-year-old Sylvia Seegrist—paused at the entrance to the mall and then pulled the trigger. When the smoke cleared, Seegrist had hit ten people, killing three of them.[12]

Seegrist had a long history of mental illness and had been previously hospitalized against her will. More recently, she had been seen many times in the mall exhibiting strange and bizarre behavior. It was no surprise to anyone when the jury found her not guilty by reason of insanity.

In a civil case, the mall management was held accountable for failing to protect its customers. In 1990, a Delaware County jury awarded an unspecified amount of money to the victims, concluding that the mall was liable for damages. The jury felt that the mall management should have stationed a trained guard at the entrance and should have attempted to commit Seegrist when she became disruptive on earlier occasions. But the management chose to do absolutely nothing.

In the 1990s, I served as an expert witness in a lawsuit against GMAC in Jacksonville, Florida, brought by its employees.[13] A down-and-out middle-aged man, James Pough, was unable to pay back the loan he had taken to purchase his 1988 Pontiac Grand Am, but that was only the beginning of his streak of bad luck. In January, Pough's wife left him. He was very much alone and thoroughly depressed. Also in January, he received a letter from GMAC indicating that the company was about to repossess his car. He turned in his Pontiac but still owed the company a total of $6,394. In March, he got another letter, this time indicating that GMAC would garnish his wages for the money he owed them.

Months later, on a Saturday night in June, Pough shot to death two people he had accused of cheating him. The next morning, he strolled into the GMAC loan office in Jacksonville, holding an AK-47 and looking to settle a score. He casually moved from office to office, shooting anything in sight. After killing eight employees, he then held a .38-caliber handgun to his head and pulled the trigger. Pough's death toll over a twenty-four-hour period was eleven, including himself.

The basis for the suit against GMAC was that the office had not been equipped with important security measures—bulletproof glass and electronic gates or even a security guard—that might have reduced Pough's body count. GMAC had many high-risk customers, some of whom had violent histories. Pough himself had been arrested on a number of occasions for vagrancy, gambling, robbery, and attempted murder. Shouldn't GMAC have anticipated an occasional problem with a disgruntled customer and have taken steps to reduce the risk of a violent episode? That is what the employees argued.

I agreed with the employees: loan companies often deal with high-risk individuals who cannot pay their bills and may have other serious personal problems. Security measures were, in my opinion, lacking. Such measures might not have totally stopped Pough's assault on GMAC, but they might have saved a few lives.

The outcome nonetheless was a loss for my side. The judge sided with GMAC rather than with its employees, arguing that security measures would not have made a difference. Maybe not, but the families of the victims will never know for sure.

Chapter 15

STIGMATIZING THE COMMUNITY

At this point in my career, I cannot help but associate a city or town with a particularly gruesome murder that occurred there. I suppose that it is inevitable, given all the slayings I've studied. It seems that whenever someone mentions their hometown, I immediately identify it with some high-profile slaying. You're from Edmond, Oklahoma? Oh, that is where Patrick Sherrill killed fifteen fellow postal workers. From Killeen, Texas? That is the site of George Hennard's mass shooting of twenty-three people who were having lunch at a local Luby's Cafeteria. You're from Littleton, Colorado? You're from Dover, Arkansas? You're from Hamilton, Ohio, or Russellville, Arkansas?

I know that these memories can be offensive, but I have trouble getting them out of my mind. Recently, I made one of my typical insensitive remarks when my wife and I visited my brother and sister-in-law in northern New Jersey. We piled into a car and drove to nearby Ridgewood for breakfast. As soon as I heard the name Ridgewood, I asked my family members whether they had heard of a post office massacre that had occurred there some years back. Ridgewood is an upper-middle-class, extremely attractive community, the last place that many would expect a brutal multiple murder to occur. And my sister-in-law's response was that I had made a mistake. Not in Ridge-wood, she said. I must be thinking of some other town.

Down the street from our destination—a popular local pancake house on North Maple Avenue—we passed by the town post office. And just in front of the building, the community had erected a memorial for the postal workers who had been slain there.

Unfortunately, I had been entirely accurate in recalling that a horrific multiple murder had occurred in the beautiful village of Ridge-wood. During the early morning hours of October 10, 1991, a fired postal worker, Joseph M. Harris, wearing a black camouflage jacket with a black ninja-type hood and carrying an arsenal of weapons, broke into the home of his ex-supervisor, Carol Ott.[1] Harris first shot her boyfriend to death as he slept in the bedroom. Finding that his handgun failed to fire on repeated attempts, he then stabbed Ott to death with a samurai sword. Harris then drove to the post office in Ridgewood, where he had been fired from his job, and killed two former coworkers. Following a lengthy standoff with the police, Harris finally surrendered and was taken into custody. He was convicted of the murders and sentenced to death but was never executed. In 1996, he was discovered unconscious in his cell. Harris was transferred to St. Frances Medical Center in Trenton, where he was pronounced dead.

I have learned a very sad lesson about the impact of a high-profile murder on the residents of a town or city—*the smaller the community, the greater the sense of identification with the murder among its residents and the greater the stigma given to the community by outsiders.* New York City is so large that even the nearly three thousand deaths that occurred there on September 11, 2001, couldn't stigmatize it. When visitors think of the Big Apple, they undoubtedly think of 9/11, but they also think of Broadway shows, Central Park, the Yankees and the Mets, countless restaurants, SoHo, former mayor Giuliani, the Empire State Building, zero-tolerance policing, the American Museum of Natural History, and a whole host of other tourist attractions. When a mass killing occurs in a small town, however, the outside world may recall only the hideous murder and nothing else.

Over the years, I have traveled to a number of cities and towns in which a multiple murder has taken place. The farthest I've traveled was to the bucolic village of Dunblane in southern Scotland, a community of some ten thousand residents located just a few miles north of Stirling. On March 13, 1996, forty-three-year-old Thomas Hamilton, a disgruntled former scout leader who had been rejected in his bid to do volunteer work with children, forced his way past school personnel and past the cafeteria into the gymnasium of Dunblane's Primary School. He opened fire on a class being held, gunning down sixteen students and their teacher.

Hamilton was legally licensed for the .357 revolver he used to massacre his victims and then to kill himself. He had long been obsessed with young boys and was profoundly resentful of his rejection by other adults in the community. Following the tragedy, parliament banned ownership of all handguns in Great Britain, but their policy change came too late for the children of Dunblane.[2]

Upon driving into Dunblane, what struck me at the time was the starkness of the contrast between the horrific crimes committed against innocent Scottish youngsters on the one hand, and on the other, the peacefulness and tranquility of this beautiful village. By the time I arrived, the Primary School had been completely refurbished and a basketball court added. Not a trace of evidence remained to suggest that the largest mass shooting in Scotland's history had occurred on the site. *Mass killings shouldn't happen anywhere, but especially not in such a peaceful setting, and especially not among children.*

A deranged and angry member of the community had been able to get a hold of a small-caliber handgun and take the lives of sixteen innocent children and a teacher. I remember thinking at the time that Hamilton might not have killed as many had all of his intended victims been adults. Someone might have fought back; others would likely have run for cover.

Of course, this tragedy occurred eleven years before thirty-two college students and faculty were shot down at Virginia Tech. Since then, I have had to revise my thinking about the ability of anyone—

even mature adults—to escape being victimized by an effective mass killer. He has the advantage: being armed to the teeth and attacking without warning. He takes advantage of the fact that mass murder is, for most people, totally inconceivable. By the time his victims realize the scope of the killer's deadly intentions, it is usually too late for anyone to escape.

When a high-profile murder occurs in a small town, it may be the only incident for which the town is ever known. The residents feel stigmatized.

The residents of Gainesville, Florida, were less than thrilled with the overwhelming presence of the media following the murder of five students at the University of Florida.[3] I remember feeling extremely uncomfortable when a television reporter from Miami began to follow me around the city as I attempted to interview members of the local community about their reactions to the gruesome murders. Many residents were fed up with the media. Others were busy evacuating the community for safer destinations, as the killer was still on the loose. Classes had been cancelled. Thousands were in the process of fleeing. And the dominant media presence only rubbed in the fact that the community was unsafe.

In Dover, Arkansas, R. Gene Simmons murdered fourteen family members in the modest home in which he lived. By the time my colleague Jamie Fox and I arrived in that town, teenagers had burned down Simmons's home. Located down a rural dirt road in a town of only a few hundred residents, the only remnants of the residence were concrete blocks that Simmons had constructed as a wall to separate his residence from the surrounding neighborhood. There was also part of a bicycle that had belonged to one of his children.

Luby's Cafeteria, site of the October 1991 massacre of twenty-three customers in Killeen, Texas, was cleaned up and reopened. But it was closed in the year 2000, perhaps because of the stigma surrounding the mass killing. The building is now the home of a Chinese buffet restaurant.

The local reaction to a hideous murder can temporarily or permanently raise the anxiety level among local residents, contribute to a circus atmosphere, or both. There is often ambivalence connected to the crime scene that repels but also attracts curious residents and visitors.

The refrigerator in which cannibal-killer Jeffrey Dahmer had stored body parts was auctioned off to the highest bidder, but who would want to live in Dahmer's apartment? When Dahmer's building was demolished, the bricks from his apartment building were sold on various Web sites.

John Wayne Gacy's single-family house at 8213 Summerdale Avenue in Des Plaines, Illinois, no longer stands.[4] He had murdered thirty-three men and boys and had buried most of the bodies in the crawl space under the house. By the time I had driven through Des Plaines and down Summerdale Avenue, Gacy's home was totally demolished by police officers who had extricated the many bodies from their burial site in the killer's basement. At least there was no longer any reason for unhappy neighbors to burn down the residence. A red-roofed house was subsequently built on the lot. But before the new residence could be constructed, gawkers would come by and urinate on the lawn, according to Lillian Grexa, "just so they could say they had urinated on John's place."[5] They also brought in a fake electric chair, which they placed conspicuously on the empty lot.

There are other more benign and helpful ways for a community to deal with the scene of especially hideous crimes. After the brutal murder of five college students in Gainesville, Florida, students at the University of Florida erected a graffiti board containing the names of the five victims. Friends and relatives of the victims left flowers at the base of the board.[6]

After the slaughter of fourteen female students at the University of Montreal Engineering School in December 1989, university administrators placed a memorial plaque containing the names of the slain students in a conspicuous place on the wall of the building. When I visited the campus a few years after the massacre, there were no other signs remaining to indicate that a heinous mass murder had occurred there.

Still, Canadians have not forgotten what many of them continue to refer to as the "crime of the century."

The Murrah Federal Building in Oklahoma City was razed after Timothy McVeigh planted explosives that took the lives of 168 people in April 1995. The site was later turned into a museum and memorial.

At the site of the 9/11 terrorist attack on the World Trade Center, New York City officials are constructing a new office tower and a memorial to the 2,749 victims of the attack.

James Huberty's rampage through a McDonald's restaurant in San Ysidro, California, resulted in the deaths of twenty-one customers and employees, mostly Latino children. The restaurant was torn down, and the land was donated to the city. Subsequently, Southwestern Community College opened its doors on the site along with a memorial to the victims.

At Columbine High in Littleton, Colorado, an atrium was constructed on the site of the library where Harris and Klebold had opened fire. A new library was built that included a memorial to the murdered students and teacher.

The tower at the University of Texas from which Charles Whitman killed fourteen and injured another thirty-one in August 1966 remained open until 1974, when four people individually jumped to their deaths. Tours of the tower are still available, but only by reservation. Still, the tower continues to be illuminated by floodlights every evening.

The reactions to massacres have been varied. At Virginia Tech, faculty, students, and administrators took positions with respect to plans for Norris Hall, the building in which twenty-five students and five professors were gunned down by Cho Seung-Hui. Built in the 1960s, Norris Hall housed the School of Engineering Science and Mechanics. Some wanted to repair the damages done by the gunman and return the building to be used again as classrooms. Others sought to make the building into a memorial for the fallen students and faculty. Still others argued to simply destroy Norris Hall. For a period of time, the site of the murders continued to be surrounded by a chain link fence. Several windows in the building remained open, their glass blown out by the gunman's bullets and by the bodies of students who sought to save themselves by jumping from a window. Some made it; some did not. Many supported renaming Norris Hall for Liviu Librescu, the engineering professor and Holocaust survivor who blocked his classroom door, allowing students to jump to safety until he was shot down by Cho. In the end, the building was reopened, but only to house engineering labs and offices. Classes will never again be held in Norris Hall.

In studying the communities in which hideous crimes have occurred, one of the first locations I visited was Hamilton, Ohio, an industrial city in which a large family massacre had occurred. Eleven people lost their lives when forty-two-year-old James Ruppert came down the stairs on Easter Sunday and shot to death his mother, Charity, his brother Leonard, his sister-in-law Alma, and his eight young nieces and nephews. At the time, Ruppert had committed the largest family mass murder in American history, but this was twelve years before R. Gene Simmons would surpass his body count.[7]

Ruppert's rampage was committed in a modest single-family home that had been occupied by James and his mother. When I arrived there some eight years after Ruppert had perpetrated the mass murder, I was surprised that the scene of his crime was still standing and that it had been sold to and was occupied by another family. Inquiring around town, I quickly determined that the new owners were from out of town and had no idea when they purchased their new residence that it had been the site of a mass slaying. I guess this is one way to sell a stigmatized property, because it is doubtful that anyone who knew about what had transpired in the house would have wanted to live there.

In 1962–1964, the Boston Strangler killed thirteen women. His first victim, Anna Slesers, age fifty-five, lived in a small apartment on the third floor off Gainsborough Street, just down the street from the Northeastern University campus where I now teach (although I was still in school in 1962). On June 14, 1962, she was sexually molested and strangled with the cord on her bathrobe. Slesers's apartment continues to be occupied by college students going to school in the Boston area, but the apartment number on the door has been changed, so as not to arouse anxiety.

When it comes to being stigmatized, the site of the Amityville Horror is a rare exception, thanks to the legendary stories that spread around the country through well-publicized fictional accounts. *The Amityville Horror* was a best-selling book published in September 1977 and was the basis of a series of motion pictures made between 1979 and 2005. On November 13, 1974, in a Dutch Colonial house at 112 Ocean Avenue, Amityville, Long Island, twenty-four-year-old Ronald DeFeo murdered the six members of his family as they slept in their beds. More than a year later, a family of five moved into the house but fled after twenty-eight days, claiming that it was haunted.[8]

Today, the residence is occupied by a family that seems to be living there without any unusual incident. The front of the home has been modified to maximize privacy. The number of the house on Ocean Avenue has been changed. But there are still visits by those who believe in the supernatural as well as other curiosity seekers.

Chapter 16

PREVENTING THE MURDEROUS IMPULSE

It seemed like back to the future, a repetition of tragic past events. While writing this book in the spring of 2007, I watched in horror as countless television newscasts featured a twenty-three-year-old student at Virginia Tech, Cho Seung-Hui, who had gone on a shooting spree on campus. Alone, he slaughtered thirty-two of his fellow students and faculty. Cho's massacre easily surpassed the body count— twelve students and a teacher—amassed in April 1999 by two bullied, alienated, and deranged students at Columbine High School in Littleton, Colorado. He also exceeded the benchmark for mass shootings established in October 1991 by George Hennard, the thirty-five-year-old man who shot to death twenty-three customers at a Luby's Cafeteria in Killeen, Texas. At that time, Hennard had the dubious distinction of being the most prolific mass shooter in American history. Unfortunately, his record body count was shattered at Virginia Tech.

The first question I always ask myself in the aftermath of a hideous killing spree is "Could this murder have been prevented?" Ironically, I had visited the campus of Virginia Tech in the picturesque town of Blacksburg some twelve months prior to the slaughter in order to give students a lecture on the characteristics of multiple murder.

More than 640 students attended. I was never able to determine whether Cho Seung-Hui was among them.

I remember being impressed at the time by the students' school spirit and their sense of community. For most students, VA Tech was a wonderful place to go to college. Even though I never interviewed the killer or got to know any of his innocent victims, the Virginia Tech mass killing became as up close and personal for me as it was for millions of Americans who hadn't known any of the victims. We all identified closely with the pain and suffering of those who had lost their lives in what can only be regarded as a senseless tragedy.

Having studied numerous mass killings for more than two decades, I looked for the warning signs that I had seen in so many previous cases. Most of them were easily located in the characteristics of the killer in Blacksburg, though, as I said earlier, many people have similar characteristics and don't perpetrate such crimes.

During the first day following the massacre, I was asked on a number of occasions to speculate about the killer's motivation. I suggested then that he was on a suicidal rampage, but before taking his own life, he had planned first to get even with everyone he held responsible for his personal miseries. Not unlike other mass murderers, the Virginia Tech killer had lived a life of depression and frustration, feeling bullied and humiliated by his peers from his early years in American schools through his senior year of high school. As an immigrant from South Korea, Cho was constantly being ridiculed from middle school on for his lack of facility with the English language and his shy disposition. Now, it was his turn to cause pain and suffering: he was looking for sweet revenge through the barrel of a semiautomatic.

Federal agents who investigated Cho's massacre suggested that he shared characteristics of a behavioral profile known as the "collector of injustice," which refers to an individual who regards any personal misery as the responsibility of others. He sees the world as being out to get him.[1] Moreover, Cho believed that people had no respect for him, and that he had to do something about it. In the end, he wrote of himself as "Ishmael," a religious figure found in the Old and New Testaments as well as the Quran who despised his brother and viewed himself as free of the control of others.

Cho left two crime scenes. In the first, he shot to death a female student and a campus adviser. Two hours passed before he showed up in the School of Engineering, where he gunned down thirty more students and faculty in four different classrooms. According to authorities, Cho chose his victims at random. Maybe, but they were random within a category. Though he targeted students and faculty at Virginia Tech, he selected a particular residence hall and a particular school on campus. Cho might have opened fire in a number of buildings, both on and off campus, but he chose not to do so. Was his selection of targets a matter of convenience? They were close by and accessible. As a student he was familiar with the classrooms and corridors. Or, was his choice of targets a result of his desire to get even with individuals who reminded him of those he believed had humiliated or ignored him?

Cho may have committed murder by proxy. Students and faculty at Virginia Tech were not his real enemies, but they would substitute nicely in his mind. The worst offenders were those students at his high school that he was convinced had bullied him on an everyday basis. They had made him feel worthless, like an outsider looking in. But they were now gone, and there was no way to gather them together in order to execute all of them collectively. On the campus of Virginia Tech, however, Cho could easily find a large number of potential victims—in classrooms around campus—who were gathered together and entirely vulnerable. He may have elected to up the body count rather than to eliminate those he detested the most.

During the two-hour interval between his attacks, Cho mailed a package of materials to NBC News containing photographs and a videotape. The photos showed him brandishing firearms, sometimes aiming them at himself and other times directing them toward others in a threatening pose. It was obvious that Cho wanted desperately to portray himself as a powerful, strong, and dangerous individual who could no longer be ignored. His videotape consisted of his "manifesto," a rambling and often incoherent diatribe in which he railed against rich people, women, and just about every other group on earth. He obviously had a need to justify his killing spree. He wanted to be seen as a victim of injustice rather than as a villain.

If he conforms to the pattern found in almost every mass killing, Cho was not a sociopath—he was not a Ted Bundy or a Ken Bianchi. He had a conscience, but he was depressed and angry. His behavior was nothing short of evil, but he wanted us to understand why he felt the need to execute his enemies.

Almost all of the warning signs found in previous mass killers could be seen in Cho's biography. He was chronically depressed and frustrated, blamed everybody but himself for his personal miseries, was socially isolated so that he had no place to turn when he got into trouble, and had access to weapons that could cause untold damage, like semiautomatics. Still, there was one missing ingredient. Unlike other mass murderers, Cho did not seem to have experienced a precipitous catastrophic loss prior to going on his rampage. Previous killers had lost a relationship as a result of a nasty separation or divorce, or had lost large amounts of money, or had been fired by a boss. Cho apparently had no known girlfriends who rejected him, hadn't flunked out of school, wasn't evicted from his apartment, and didn't seem to be in need of a job.

Yet there was one tremendous loss that was imminent in Cho's life. He was only weeks away from graduation. As bad as his life had been on campus, it might have been dramatically worse after he graduated. Like many other college seniors, Cho may have felt extremely anxious about leaving the structured life of a college student to be on his own. As a twenty-three-year-old senior, he would finally be asked to grow up, be a responsible adult, and find his own way in life. Most likely, he would be considered too old to live off his family and would find it necessary to move from his home on campus. I doubt that he felt capable of fending for himself.

The transition to adulthood is hard enough even for those fortunate college students who have friends and are accepted by their peers;

many normal college students are ambivalent about graduating. The suicide rate among college students peaks during their senior year, at the very time you might think they would be most happy about possibilities for the future.[2] But the transition is that much harder for a person like Cho, who was already on the edge, holding onto his sanity by a thread. He must have felt that he was about to be kicked off the campus, and, in a sense, that is exactly true of all those students who receive their diplomas. It is time to leave, whether they like it or not.

As noted earlier, warning signs usually do not help to identify a killer before he attacks. We simply cannot predict, based on any profile, who will and who will not turn out to commit a massacre. Hundreds of thousands of students—and many others—may feel wronged and alienated but would never kill anyone. Are we to lock away countless innocent people based on what they *might* do?

In the case of students who exhibit warning signs, we should be helping them to become better adjusted. We should be using these red flags to identify troubled students long before they become troublesome—not to punish them, but to give them a helping hand. If we wait until a student has murderous intentions, there may be little if anything we can do to stop him. Recognizing that Cho was a threat, one instructor at Virginia Tech tried to get him into therapy, but he refused to go. From Cho's viewpoint, why should he get counseling when he was the only sane student on campus? Cho may have reasoned: *Let my instructor get therapy; give it to my classmates. They are all crazy, not me!*

If someone had intervened years earlier, however, the killer might have been willing to accept the help that he needed. But until Cho looked threatening—until he began stalking women and revealing his violent fantasies in class—he was pretty much ignored. Warning signs are effective, but not to identify a budding mass murderer, which is close to impossible. We should use these signs to intervene as early as possible because we want to improve the quality of life for all of our students. In the process, we might even prevent the next mass killing.

One other thing about the Virginia Tech massacre deserves to be mentioned. I don't think it is an accident that it happened in a town like Blacksburg, Virginia. The community of Blacksburg looks and feels very much like most of the towns in which school shootings have occurred since 1996. Blacksburg joins the ranks of obscure and out-of-the-way places like Pearl, West Paducah, Jonesboro, Edinburgh, Littleton, Moses Lake, and Bethel. In such towns, most residents do indeed share a strong sense of community, but young people who feel like outsiders looking in—those who have been ignored or rejected by others—have few if any alternatives for sources of companionship and self-esteem. If they don't fit into mainstream campus life, they simply don't fit in anywhere locally. Thus, they may feel trapped in a terrible situation. Some students on the Virginia Tech campus apparently did attempt to reach out to Cho, but he refused to reciprocate in kind. But by the time he became a college freshman, it may already have been too late to help him.

In the days and weeks following the Virginia Tech massacre, there were copycat threats and hoaxes in high schools and on college campuses around the country. We expect that young people will always identify with the suffering of the victims of a publicized murder, and the vast majority do. But a few—those who resemble the killer with respect to his marginal and alienated position among his peers—will see themselves in the killer's shoes. Some will be inspired to imitate what they regard as heroic behavior. If a middle school student goes on a rampage, it would probably not have much influence on college students. Few would take their cue from someone so much younger. But when a college student commits a mass murder, it has a great impact on middle and high school students for whom college is an important objective: college students are role models. In the aftermath of the publicity given to the Virginia Tech massacre, two high school students in Colorado Springs were arrested for plotting to kill a record number of their schoolmates. Their plan was to become famous by murdering more than thirty-three students, a warped desire to beat the record established by Cho at Virginia Tech.

College campuses continue to be among the safest locations in our society. There are some seventeen million college students, and typically only a few of them become homicide victims every year: while studying in the library, sleeping in their dorms, or attending a lecture. They are much more likely to be victimized once they have left the campus—on the streets, in a bar, on public transportation, or even at home.

Nonetheless, the Virginia Tech massacre reminds us that there have been some bloody exceptions in institutions of higher learning in both Canada and the United States.

As mentioned earlier, on August 1, 1966, Eagle Scout and college student Charles Whitman shot to death fourteen people from his platform atop the Texas Tower on the campus of the University of Texas in Austin. He also wounded another thirty-one before he was finally gunned down by a civilian sharpshooter.

On May 4, 1970, four students were shot to death by National Guard soldiers who had been called in to put down a student protest on the campus of Ohio's Kent State University.

On July 12, 1976, Edward Charles Allaway, a janitor working in the library on the campus of California State University in Fullerton, fatally shot seven of his coworkers who he incorrectly believed had forced his estranged wife to appear in pornographic films.

In 1978, Theodore Streleski, a doctoral candidate in mathematics at Stanford University, bludgeoned to death his faculty adviser with a ball-peen hammer. Streleski had been a doctoral student for some nineteen years and felt that his professors had unfairly held back on granting his degree.

On December 26, 1989, Mark Lepine, a twenty-five-year-old man who had been rejected from the University of Montreal School of Engineering, walked into a classroom there holding an AK-47. First, he asked all the male students to leave and then opened fire on the women, killing fourteen of them. Lepine blamed "feminists" for all of his personal problems.

On November 1, 1991, twenty-eight-year-old Gang Lu, who had recently received a doctorate in physics, opened fire on students and faculty members in two buildings on the campus of the University of Iowa. He killed five and injured two more before taking his own life. Lu's motive? Revenge for the fact that he had been denied an academic award that would have landed him a good job. One of his victims was the student who had bested him for the honor.

In September 1992, fifty-one-year-old Valery Fabrikant, an engineer and researcher, was fired from his faculty position at Concordia University in Montreal. Almost a year later, he came back to campus with an arsenal of weapons to get even. In the process, Fabrikant took the lives of four professors and a secretary in the department of mechanical engineering.

On August 15, 1996, Frederick Davidson, a thirty-six-year-old graduate student at San Diego State University, shot to death three of his professors during a hearing where he was unsuccessfully defending his doctoral dissertation.

On August 28, 2000, James Kelly, a thirty-six-year-old graduate student at the University of Arkansas, gunned down his faculty adviser after learning that he had been dropped from the doctoral program in English.

On January 16, 2002, a forty-two-year-old student who had failed to graduate from Virginia's Appalachian School of Law came back to campus where he took the lives of a student, a professor, and a dean.

On October 28, 2002, three faculty members in the University of Arizona's College of Nursing were shot down by forty-year-old Robert Flores, who was being dropped from his course of study as a result of failing grades. The Gulf War veteran then took his own life.

On September 2, 2006, forty-nine-year-old Douglas Pennington killed his two sons and himself while visiting the campus of Shepherd University in Shephardstown, West Virginia. Mental illness was named as the motive. In a suicide note, Pennington took responsibility for killing his sons but suggested that he only wanted to spare them the suffering they would surely experience in this life.

On September 13, 2007, Kimveer Gill from the town of Laval, near Montreal, wearing a black trench coat, opened fire on students at

Dawson College in Montreal, shooting twenty of them, including one young woman who later died.

At Lincoln-Sudbury Regional, a high school west of Boston, a sixteen-year-old student allegedly stabbed to death a fifteen-year-old schoolmate he hardly knew.[3] The suspect had long been the victim of bullying and humiliating remarks by fellow students who saw his behavior as weird. He was belittled for wearing a trench coat like the ones worn by the Columbine High School teenagers who killed twelve students and a teacher in Littleton, Colorado. The suspect hadn't been drinking; he had no criminal record. But he had taken several prescription medications, including an antidepressant. Moreover, when it was determined that the suspect had been diagnosed with Asperger's syndrome, a mild form of autism, his affliction and the treatment for it became the focal point of almost every press and television report. There was little discussion of the impact of constant bullying—being teased, ridiculed, even threatened on a daily basis, a common denominator among students around the nation who have sought revenge against their classmates. There was also almost no talk of policies and programs to break the culture of silence and encourage students to report threatening behavior. Rather than deal with issues at school that might help to prevent deadly violence in the future, everybody seemed to prefer focusing on a characteristic of the killer that might never be found in school murders again—his affliction with autism.

After a tragic murder occurs, there is almost always an unproductive attempt to place the blame where it will do absolutely nothing to prevent the problem from occurring again. Blame his parents, blame his medication, blame his mental illness, blame the school. A much more constructive approach would be to examine aspects of the school structure that might be changed to discourage a repetition of would-be murderous students acting out through violence.

In schools around the country, some principals and superintendents have responded to the Columbine-type killings by incorporating antibullying programs into their curricular and extracurricular activities. There are now many effective methods for increasing student empathy for the victims of bullying, for bringing harassed students into the mainstream, for encouraging teachers and school psychologists to take bullying seriously, and for intervening when a student is constantly being ridiculed and humiliated. *Bullying has been a part of student culture for centuries. It is about time we treat it as what it is: not something to be overlooked or tolerated, but a cancer that should be removed from all of our schools.*

A middle school principal in a Boston suburb recently complained that the *real* obstacle to ending bullying is that even the victims and their parents are caught up in the culture of silence. Drawing from her personal experiences as a school administrator, she said that she is seldom contacted by parents of bullied victims, no matter how much she cajoles them to do so. Instead, students and their parents are generally unwilling to report any episode of bullying. They refuse to cooperate with school administrators or they ask her to back off and do absolutely nothing. Her advice to parents? Stop teaching children that it is wrong to be a tattletale. Help school administrators and teachers to break the culture of silence.

It is not only a few school shooters who are being ignored and isolated. We Americans generally suffer from a shrinking sense of community. This trend is represented in the title of Professor Robert Putnam's book *Bowling Alone*, which can be taken literally—fewer people are bowling in groups or organizations.[4] But the book's title is also a metaphor for the much larger issue of vast loneliness in American society. As I mentioned earlier, many states—especially California, Florida, Texas, Alaska, Illinois, and New York—have an abundance of strangers; individuals who have moved hundreds, perhaps thousands, of miles for the sake of a new beginning or a last resort. Not coincidentally, these states also have more than their share of mass and serial killings. Moreover, even in areas where a sense of community exists, there are always some individuals who don't fit in. When students first arrive on college campuses around the country, they are total strangers to one another. Some make the adjustment with ease; others remain isolated. And, as noted earlier, those who feel alienated in out-of-the-way places have fewer avenues to find companionship and support.

Growing numbers of Americans do not have a good support system in place. As a result, they have no place to turn when they get into trouble; they lack family and friends who might give them the encouragement and support they so desperately desire. A very few will solve their problems through the barrel of a gun with tragic results. We must try to stop this from happening. We can do a better job of reaching out to those individuals who are obviously in need of assistance. It isn't only children who cry out for help; many adult Americans are troubled but have no place to turn for support.

Teenagers are especially in need of attention, yet, for too many years, we have asked millions of our youngsters to raise themselves— and too many haven't done a very good job. Teenagers who commit acts of violence for the sadistic thrill are looking to gain some control over their own lives. Just like school shooters, they want desperately to feel important. The last thing they want is to be ignored. This is the issue to address if we, as a society, want to bring about a long-term, permanent decline in the juvenile murder rate.

Gangs give many youngsters everything missing from their everyday lives. Gang membership provides a sense of family, a social bond, allies in a threatening environment, and a feeling of importance, of being special. Moreover, gangs are connected to the illicit drug trade, wherein young people can make lots of money over a short period of time. Gangs are also increasingly being associated with murders.

We should be giving our teenagers healthy alternatives to violence and hate, so they feel good about themselves when they do the right thing. They need adult supervision; they need to have hope for the future. There is a crying need to generate more summer jobs that might lead to a viable career; more athletic programs; more music, drama, and art; more quality after-school programs, internships, and community centers; more parents, teachers, and college students who volunteer to tutor in the schools. When middle-class opportunities for success seem attainable, gang membership loses much of its appeal. When access to legitimate opportunities is a reality, hate and violence lose their glamour and the murder rate spirals downward.

Moreover, we should reach out to children who appear to be at risk long before they look like budding serial killers or sadistic rapists and murderers. Young children who show dysfunctional signs should be given help as early as possible. The objective of sadism is to achieve a sense of power and dominance. There is no realistic way to rehabilitate a sadistic sociopath who has made a career of killing. A forty-two-year-old repeat rapist or murderer doesn't suddenly develop a conscience. He may find religion, shed tears, say all the right things, but chances are, he is no more remorseful now than he was when he raped or killed for the pleasure of it.

The earlier we intervene to help a young person who feels a profound sense of powerlessness, the more effective we will be.

Chapter 17

RESPONDING TO THE MURDEROUS IMPULSE

It is essential that we intervene early in the lives of budding serial killers and would-be sadistic murderers and rapists to prevent them from realizing their destructive potential. If we choose to intervene effectively, the same rule ought to apply to how we respond to a growing presence of violent crime.

I am not suggesting that we treat juvenile offenders as though they were adults. There is much evidence that teenagers are developmentally different from grown-ups in significant ways. I believe that many adolescent offenders are "temporary sociopaths," with the emphasis on "temporary." They might perpetrate an act of criminal violence at the age of fifteen that they wouldn't dream of committing if and when they reach the age of twenty-five. Yet, in too many cases, under-age burglars and drug addicts are nowadays being tried as adults and given lengthy prison sentences. This is true despite research by criminologists showing that the recidivism rate is significantly higher among teenagers who are tried as adults rather than as juveniles.[1]

On the other hand, it is just as important that we not give juvenile offenders merely a slap on the wrist. There are meaningful lessons to be learned from examining strategies and tactics that were applied effectively during the mid-1990s to bring down the juvenile murder rate. In major cities around the country, clergy, parents, neighbors,

187

probation officers, and the police collaborated to identify and punish incorrigible youngsters who had contributed most to the surge of violence and seemed clearly beyond redemption. The effort was two-pronged: prevention programs that reached out to local teenagers with supervision and guidance as well as a law-and-order approach that took the worst youthful offenders off the streets and incarcerated them in a juvenile facility.[2]

At the same time, police officers were placed conspicuously in high-crime areas in order to keep a watchful eye on the neighborhood. In one or another version of community policing, officers left their patrol cars and walked a beat, increasing their visibility and their interaction with residents. In the long run, community policing—in which officers collaborate with residents in their crime-fighting efforts—helped to stem the tide of murder in cities across the country. This is not the confrontational and aggressive policing often identified with a "zero-tolerance" policy, but it is based on increasing the cooperation between residents and law enforcement.

A police presence is, of course, not the only effective strategy for responding to the violence perpetrated by young people. Installing surveillance cameras in crime hot spots can have a supplemental deterrent effect, but only when crime-prone youngsters understand that they are likely to be identified and apprehended. It is therefore essential to publicize the presence of monitoring devices.

Some object to the presence of cameras based on concerns over a perceived loss of privacy and civil liberties. But they should be reminded that the cameras are placed in public spaces, not inside of homes or apartments or community centers or churches.

Most European countries now employ public video surveillance to discourage crime, drugs, and terrorism. More than 1.5 million closed-circuit television systems monitor the streets and roads of English cities and towns. Perpetrators of the aborted terrorist attacks on the London Underground at the end of July 2005 were later identified and apprehended, thanks to the presence of surveillance cameras located in London's train stations.[3]

Although they are much less prevalent, public surveillance cameras in the United States have aided in bringing violent criminals to justice. In June 2007, twenty-six-year-old Edwin Hall was charged with abducting and murdering eighteen-year-old Kelsey Smith. The victim was accosted in the parking lot of a Target department store in Overland Park, Kansas, where she had gone to shop for a gift for her boyfriend. Four days later, her body was discovered some twenty miles away, near a lake in a park across the state line in Missouri.

Kelsey Smith's disappearance might have been treated as just one more missing person's report if it hadn't been for the presence of cameras in Target's parking lot. During the search for the teenager, local police publicly released two videos. The first showed her leaving the store at about the same time as a young man of slight build, wearing a goatee. The second showed Smith being forced into a car in the parking lot. A neighbor called the police after recognizing Edwin Hall in the video, and he was arrested.

Many cities have imposed a late-night curfew in order to reduce violent crimes committed by young people. The only problem with curfews is the lack of evidence that they actually work. During the 1990s, for example, San Jose imposed a nighttime curfew at the same time that San Francisco eliminated its curfew. Both had rising crime rates. San Jose's law had no effect on teenage crime; San Francisco's juvenile crime rate plummeted.[4] Adults tend to commit crimes in the dead of night; teenagers commit a disproportionate number of offenses in the afternoon—after the school bell rings and before Mom and Dad come home from work. It might be effective to place a 10 p.m. curfew on adults, but not on the younger crowd.

One of the most critical lessons I have learned from conducting decades of research is that *the public can be effectively involved in bringing a murderer to justice.* This is not to suggest that people engage in vigilantism. The defendant accused of the kidnapping murder of Kelsey Smith, as was just noted, was apprehended as a result of a tip from the public. And it is unfortunate that the police sometimes do not fully appreciate the need for the public's participation. During an investigation, law enforcement officials often unnecessarily limit the information they are willing to release and fail to encourage the public's cooperation. Of course, there are times in an investigation when evidence should be held close to the vest. For example, in order to exclude false confessors, certain aspects of the crime scene that only the killer would know might be kept secret. Yet I have found that investigators too often withhold important information from the public, even when there is no sensible reason for doing so.

In November 2006, just outside of Atlantic City, the bodies of four prostitutes were discovered dumped in a ditch located behind a string of cheap motels on the outskirts of town. All of the corpses were positioned facedown, clothed but barefoot, their heads pointing east toward the casinos and boardwalk. There was little doubt that all four victims had been killed by the same person. But very little news about the investigation was forthcoming from police investigators.

When prostitutes are victimized, there is little pressure on the police to solve the crime and find the killer. Many view this type of crime as criminals killing criminals, not criminals murdering respectable middle-class citizens. Moreover, many prostitutes are disconnected from their family and old friends, so it may take a good deal of time before anyone notices that these women are missing, let alone dead.

The prevailing wisdom may also be that drawing too much attention to a serial killer who operates in a certain community can adversely impact local business. This may be especially true for areas like Atlantic City, whose economy depends so much on drawing tourists to the casinos. Thus, no information about the murdered prostitutes was given on the county Web site; only a muted response was forthcoming from the police chief and mayor about the crimes.

It is enlightening to compare the reticence of the police in the United States with the greater willingness of law enforcement in England to share information with the public. Some sixty miles northeast of London, near the town of Ipswich, a serial killer recently took the lives of five prostitutes over a ten-day period. An investigation was quickly begun, involving five hundred police officers and thirty-six departments around the country. The local authorities immediately began to post press releases on the county Web site, thirty in all. They asked the public to cooperate by turning in any discarded clothing that might have belonged to one of the victims. The police distributed thousands of flyers containing information about taking precautions to maintain personal safety. Prime Minister Tony Blair conveyed his sympathies to the family of the murdered women. County law enforcement received more than eleven thousand phone calls from the public.

We should trust the public to do the right thing under the right conditions. In the Ipswich murders, a suspect was arrested and charged on December 21; in Atlantic City, the case continues to be unsolved.

Being tightlipped about a serial murder can also delay closing the case. The problem is that individuals are usually willing to identify a suspect in their midst, but only if they are given enough information to feel fairly sure that the person they are turning in really committed the crime. Most people do not need a large reward; they simply want to be good citizens by bringing a killer to justice. Unless there is reason to bring a case into the spotlight, it is cynical and may be counterproductive to offer hundreds of thousands, even millions of dollars for information leading to the arrest of a murderer. This strategy brings every pathological liar out of the woodwork, yielding to the investigators a large number of misleading and irrelevant tips.

Perhaps partially as a result of the $500,000 reward offered, the task force in the 2002 DC Sniper murders received more than sixty thousand tips from members of the public who phoned the tip hotline. There were so many phone calls that they couldn't possibly be managed or prioritized. In fact, the tip line operator hung up four times on one of the actual murderers, believing his phone calls to be a hoax. He wanted to negotiate with Chief Moose to stop killing in exchange for $10,000,000. Instead, Malvo and Muhammad left written messages at their crime scenes and continued their killing spree. Still, it was a tip from the public that finally led to the apprehension of the DC Snipers. Whitney Donahue of Greencastle, Pennsylvania, phoned the police after noticing the two asleep in their blue Chevrolet Caprice in a rest area off of Route 95 in Frederick County, Maryland.

In addition to murderous snipers, I have studied many serial killers and sadistic murderers and rapists who have preyed on children. Predators such as Joseph Edward Duncan III, who bludgeoned to death three people in northern Idaho and kidnapped two children, killing one of them, represents a tremendous challenge to the criminal justice system. What are we to do with a dangerous sex offender who has served his sentence but is likely to repeat his offense?

Duncan had served a fifteen-year sentence in a Washington State prison for raping a fourteen-year-old boy and was out on bail for molesting a six-year-old boy. For every repeat offender who turns his life around, there are others who commit even more hideous crimes. Many sex offenders attack dozens of children before they are finally arrested. That is why the official reports of relatively low recidivism rates for pedophiles may be somewhat misleading. Still, the evidence is also clear that not every sex offender has an *uncontrollable* urge— an obsession—to molest and assault our children. When the intervention is early and effective, there are some sex offenders who can be rehabilitated.

Legislators around the country have recently devoted much time to writing tougher laws to track, restrict, or sentence dangerous rapists and child molesters. While well-intentioned, almost all such legislation is sadly bound to fail.[5]

Megan's Law, which began in New Jersey, mandates that sex offenders register with law enforcement authorities when they are released from prison and makes provisions for residents to be notified when a dangerous sex offender moves nearby. The 1994 law originated out of the sincere concerns of a grieving family in suburban Trenton, whose daughter Megan Kanka was sexually assaulted and murdered by a convicted sex offender who was living across the street. Megan's Law has been a model for dozens of state laws across the country and for a federal version passed by Congress two years later. Many parents are convinced of the effectiveness of Megan's Law. Who wouldn't want to know that a dangerous sex offender is living next door?

The only problem is there is little if any evidence that Megan's Law has reduced the likelihood of children being victimized by dangerous pedophiles. Even worse, there is reason to believe that it might actually encourage recidivism among sex offenders in the community who might otherwise have made an effort to behave themselves.

Many sex offenders never register with the police, preferring to risk being sent back to prison rather than to endure the stigma that might very well destroy their lives. Those who have registered, as mandated by law, may suffer the consequences. As soon as the word gets around, they are evicted from their apartments, lose their jobs, and are humiliated or even threatened by the neighbors.

Feeling out of options in the legitimate sector, the offender may be thrown back into a criminal circle. He may come to think that it is much easier to rob, cheat, and steal than to rely on a community that despises him. Even worse, some stigmatized and rejected offenders may take up where they left off before being incarcerated, their weak internal controls being taxed to the limit by a policy that only separates them from the social controls they so desperately need. Joseph Duncan was a registered sex offender; it didn't stop him from committing murder.

More and more communities are imposing buffer zones to keep a distance between sex offenders and the schools. The problem is that children are everywhere, not just in the schools. They are in daycare centers, at bus stops, in front yards playing with friends, in shopping malls, at zoos, at swimming pools, in churches, and on playgrounds. Many buffer zones are so large that they cover the entire town or city in which they are imposed. A registered sex offender who wants to obey the law may have no choice but to give up his life in a community and move to another town or city, where he is likely again to be evicted, be fired, and face humiliation from his neighbors. In many cases, the ex-con may live in the same residence with children—perhaps his own children or those of his partner. Or, if he is on his own, he may end up in a homeless shelter. A 2007 *Boston Globe* review of seventy-seven high-risk sex offenders in the city of Boston, men who had sexually assaulted children or women, found that most of them—some two-thirds—reported they were living in a shelter. Around the country, this is the rule rather than the exception.[6]

Shelters may seem like a last resort for offenders who have been evicted from a number of communities where they have registered or have been limited by buffer zones. Yet towns across the country have recently also declared shelters off-limits to registered pedophiles. The realistic last resort may consist of sex offenders living as homeless people under a bridge or on the streets, where nobody is around to keep an eye on them—where they are completely without supervision. The question is, does the community approach—offender registries and buffer zones—actually pull sex offenders out of the mainstream and push them back into a life of violent crime? One thing is clear: many of these former criminals are not being integrated into the community.

States like Florida and Oklahoma have passed laws requiring the use of electronic monitors that apply Global Positioning System technology for tracking sexual predators in the community. Legislatures in a number of other states are now considering the same. Jessica's Law—named after a Florida girl who was abducted, sexually assaulted, and brutally murdered—mandates that first-time sexual predators who have completed their prison sentences wear an electronic ankle bracelet for life.

In theory, electronic bracelets would help law enforcement to keep an eye on high-risk offenders who come close to places where children congregate. This measure would, in all likelihood, help to prosecute sex offenders who violate the terms of their parole, but it would hardly prevent them from committing new offenses. Even Martha Stewart, who received a sentence of home confinement for her insider-trading violation, claims to have been able to dismantle her electronic monitoring bracelet.[7] To this point, electronic monitoring has worked successfully for discouraging low-level offenders—burglars, embezzlers, and drug dealers, but not dedicated sex offenders—from repeating their crimes. It would be an unmanageable task for authorities to monitor the hundreds of thousands of offenders who would wear such devices.

Recognizing that buffer zones, registries, and electronic monitoring do not provide the answer, states are now seeking methods for keeping dangerous sex offenders incarcerated after they have served their time and are scheduled for release. In January 2002, the Supreme Court ruled that dangerous inmates could be held indefinitely, but only if they are proven to lack the capacity for controlling their sexually harmful behavior; that is, they must suffer from some mental disorder.

The problem with this approach is twofold: First, many sexual predators have personality disorders and are not considered to be seriously ill. They choose to do the wrong thing because they enjoy it, and so they are ineligible for indefinite incarceration. Second, psychiatrists and psychologists (not to mention criminologists) working for the state must decide who deserves continued incarceration, but can even they effectively predict dangerous behavior? How can we depend on them to determine who is returned to the community and who remains behind bars?

Question: If a sex offender is proven to be dangerous, why should he be in anybody's neighborhood? Why should he be released from prison and returned to the community at any time or under any condition?

As long as the community approach continues to stigmatize those repeat sex offenders who have been released into the community, there is really only one way for the criminal justice system to protect our children from sexual predators: *Make sure they are separated from the rest of us.*

I am not talking about a middle-aged man who urinates in the park or an eighteen-year-old who has committed statutory rape by having consensual sex with an underage (15-year-old) boy or girl. *But dangerous* repeat *offenders should be given the life sentences they deserve.*

It seems better for everyone, certainly for children and for the offenders themselves, to incarcerate them for life. Perhaps certain youthful first offenders should receive a limited sentence behind bars, under the assumption that many of them could be rehabilitated if given the chance. But for the repeat offender who has committed a heinous crime against children—murder, rape, assault, kidnapping—there should be only one response: *Two strikes and you are never out again.*

There are many people who believe that even a life sentence is too soft for sadistic rapists and murderers, that we ought to reserve capital punishment for the serial killers and sadistic murderers profiled in this book. I am not so sure.

Whenever I articulate my opposition to the death penalty, I feel like a voice in the wilderness. More than 65 percent of all Americans favor the death penalty, and the remaining 35 percent would probably be willing to make an exception if it meant eliminating the Jeffrey Dahmers and Clifford Olsons of the world. In fact, the United States has the dubious distinction of being the only remaining Western nation not to have abolished the death penalty for civil homicide.

Actually, support for the death penalty has decreased somewhat since the mid-1990s, when 80 percent of all Americans were in favor of executing murderers. Not coincidentally, during this period of time, we were just coming off an unprecedented increase in the murder rate, and Americans were desperate to find a solution. In 1966, when the homicide rate had not yet skyrocketed, the death penalty received support from only 42 percent of all Americans. Americans still felt safe.[8]

Yet increases and decreases in the rate of homicide explain only a part of changing attitudes toward executing criminals. More Americans are now aware of the mistakes that have been made in administering the death penalty. In addition, many people continue to support capital punishment simply because they are skeptical about whether inmates will actually remain incarcerated for the rest of their lives.

Some proponents of capital punishment assert that legislators should enact death penalty laws because it is the will of the people. Well, it is true that the majority of Americans support capital punishment—*but only* if they are not given an alternative that they like better. When they are offered an option to capital punishment, such as life without parole, their support for the death penalty drops to 50 percent, even lower when you throw in compensating the victim's family.

Unfortunately, many of our citizens really aren't informed enough about existing penalties to make an informed decision about crime and punishment. In one survey, pollsters found that only a fraction of the residents of Massachusetts—about 3 percent—even knew that the Commonwealth's penalty for first-degree murder was life without parole. One-third of all Massachusetts citizens said they believed such offenders would be out of prison in less than ten years; another 11 percent said they had no idea at all what happened to first-degree murderers in the state.

Many people ask why we should spend hard-earned taxpayer money to imprison a murderer when we could just as easily execute him at a much lower cost. But the fixed costs of running a maximum-security prison are little affected by the presence of a few additional inmates serving life sentences for first-degree murder. The warden still has to be paid and the heat still has to be kept on.

Moreover, because of the amount of pretrial time required, the large number of expert witnesses, the massive amount of evidence presented, the number of attorneys appointed for both the defense and prosecution, the increased need to sequester the jury, and the lengthy appeals process required by the Supreme Court in capital cases, it actually costs less to imprison a killer than to execute one. Death penalty trials take three to five times longer than typical murder trials. In Florida, for example, the average case that results in execution has traditionally cost $3.2 million, whereas the estimated cost of imprisonment for forty years was slightly more than $500,000. In Texas, a death penalty case now costs an average of $2.3 million, whereas the cost of imprisoning someone in a cell for forty years is less than $800,000. In North Carolina, the cost per execution is $216,000 more than the cost of a non–death penalty trial imposing a sentence of life imprisonment. In California, the cost per execution is now $250,000,000.

Proponents of the death penalty also claim that it deters violent criminals. They believe we need to execute murderers to send messages to potential killers that, if they can't control their murderous behavior, the same thing will happen to them. Yet the death penalty has little if any effect on killings. In an early study of fourteen nations in which the death penalty was eliminated, criminologists Dane Archer and Rosemary Gartner report, for example, that abolition was followed more often than not by a reduction in national homicide rates.[9] For example, homicide dropped 59 percent in Finland, 30 percent in Italy, 63 percent in Sweden, and 46 percent in Switzerland. In only five of these fourteen countries did homicide increase at all.

Even more ironic, research conducted by criminologist William Bowers suggests that the murder rate actually increases for a short period after the killer has been executed, producing what he calls a brutalization effect.[10] That is, would-be murderers apparently identify more with the state executioner than they do with the inmate. In other words, they are inspired to imitate, in their own personal behavior, the state's version of attaining justice.

In his 2005 testimony to the New York State Assembly Standing Committee on Codes, criminologist Jeffrey Fagan summarized the prevailing thinking among his colleagues.[11] Overall, the existing research fails to support the deterrent effect of capital punishment. The several recent studies supporting the death penalty fail to achieve scientific acceptability. Their claims of a deterrent effect fall apart under close scrutiny. In particular, they are weighed down in technical and conceptual errors, they use inappropriate statistical methods, they fail to include all of the important factors that influence the rate of murder, and they do not provide a direct test of deterrence. In sum, "[t]here is no reliable, scientifically sound evidence that execution can exert an effect that either acts separately or sufficiently powerfully to overwhelm . . . [the] consistent and recurring epidemic patterns [of murder over time]."[12]

Another widely held argument, of course, is that capital punishment protects society by guaranteeing that inmates like Charles Manson will never be paroled. And, certainly, capital punishment ensures that particular murderers never kill again. But before I support the death penalty, I want to know whether an alternative exists for protecting society—for making sure that a killer isn't granted another opportunity—without the state's taking a human life. If the alternative in response to a brutal, hideous murder is life imprisonment with parole eligibility, then I am indeed in favor of the death penalty. If, however, the alternative is a life sentence without the possibility of ever being paroled, then capital punishment becomes unnecessary for the protection of society, and I am therefore against it.

In fact, I cringe whenever I hear that Charles Manson is being considered for parole, because I know what people will say: The criminal justice system is soft on murderers. We should be executing those who commit heinous crimes.

Actually, Charles Manson did receive the death penalty. But in 1972, the Supreme Court struck down capital punishment because it was being applied in an uneven, capricious manner. At that point, murderers on death row were given the next most severe sentence under state law. In California, that sentence was a life sentence with parole eligibility. As a result, Charles Manson was then eligible for parole after serving only seven years.

A series of rulings by the Supreme Court in 1976 paved the way for states to restore the death penalty, but only when it was applied under strict guidelines. In some states, those convicted of murder continue to become eligible for parole after serving only several years in prison; but if the court adds the special circumstances provision, the only possible sentences are either death or life imprisonment without parole eligibility.

Most states now have special circumstances statutes for heinous crimes, such as multiple murder or murder with rape. In some states (e.g., Massachusetts), all first-degree murderers are ineligible for parole, so that no special statute is required. Under such conditions, the death penalty is unnecessary as a means for protecting society from vicious killers, because we can instead lock them up and throw away the key.

It is also true that we have made a large number of mistakes in administering the death penalty. More than one hundred innocent people have in all probability been condemned to die. This recognition recently led the former governor of Illinois—a staunch advocate of capital punishment—to declare a moratorium on the death penalty until such time that the state is comfortable that it is not executing innocent people.

The standard for applying the death penalty needs to be strengthened. Taking someone's life is irreversible, it should require more than a jury's deciding on the defendant's guilt "beyond a reasonable doubt." Before we execute anyone, we should insist that jurors have no doubt at all. Under an absolute standard, of course, we probably wouldn't ever administer the death penalty, but we also wouldn't make any mistakes.

On May 16, 2007, in Elizabeth, New Jersey, forty-six-year-old Byron Halsey, an inmate who served more than twenty years in prison for raping and killing two children, finally had his conviction thrown out, thanks to a DNA analysis indicating that the victims' neighbor may have been responsible. In 1988, Halsey had been convicted three years earlier of sexually assaulting and murdering these two children—his girlfriend's children—ages seven and eight, in a Plainfield rooming house. They had all been living there together. The bodies of the young victims were discovered in the basement of their residence.

At the time of the original trial, the evidence seemed to point to Halsey as the killer. But the recent DNA test suggested instead that another resident of the rooming house was the real source of the semen found at the crime scene. The neighbor who is now under suspicion is presently serving a prison sentence for sex offenses he committed during the early 1990s. He had testified against Halsey at his trial twenty years ago.

DNA testing has recently been used to confirm the guilt or innocence of inmates on death row who continue to proclaim their innocence. The problem is that murderers don't always—or even usually—

leave their DNA at the crime scene. Moreover, there are scandalous conditions at some state crime labs around the country, making it difficult to rely on the results of DNA analysis or even fingerprint evidence.

Some believe we should save the death penalty for only the most heinous crimes, especially sadistic serial murders. As we have seen, however, there are serious ambiguities about the guilt or innocence of those convicted of committing the worst sorts of crimes. Convicted killer Doug Clark is on death row, but he blames almost everything on his partner, Carol Bundy, and he makes a fairly strong case for himself. Which pathological liar should the court have believed? Clifford Olson, who raped and murdered children in British Columbia, falsely confesses to murders in order to up his bodycount. He enjoys the perception that he is a real-life Hannibal Lecter. How many false confessors are there on death row? Male nurse Orville Lynn Majors was convicted of poisoning to death six hospital patients. He continues to argue that they were not poisoned but died of natural causes. In a hosptial setting, there are always unexplained deaths that may be linked with the medical reasons for admitting patients in the first place. Even an autopsy doesn't always turn up definitive evidence one way or another—whether death by murder or natural causes. And Ken Bianchi is regarded as a manipulative sociopath. Is it possible that he was really the psychotic multiple personality portrayed by defense psychologists? If so, he should be in a hospital, not behind bars serving a life sentence. In the absence of his plea bargain whereby he testified against his cousin Angelo, Bianchi would in all likelihood have been executed. Pamela Smart continues to argue that her fifteen-year-old lover was exclusively to blame for the shooting death of her husband. It was his idea and not hers to execute her husband, Gregg. Similarly, Charles Manson maintains that he never gave the order to take the lives of Sharon Tate and six others. And how are we to know definitively that either one of them—Pamela Smart or Charles Manson—is not telling the truth? If we cannot be certain about the guilt or innocence of such notorious convicted murderers, how is it possible to apply the death penalty with total accuracy to the range of prisoners on death row, many of whom are there based on eyewitness testimony, which has proven to be highly unreliable?

It is of paramount importance that we understand the characteristics of the murderers who perpetrate the worst kinds of violence. We must also ask ourselves what can be done to cause a reduction in their ranks. Are these grotesque offenses relatively rare? Perhaps. Are these kinds of crimes widely known? Yes. Yet such killers are generally understood superficially or misunderstood altogether. It is my hope that these pages will provide clarity to the public's perception of serial killers and other vicious murderers so we can better devise laws and strategies to combat and capture them, and perhaps even deter them from following that path.

In conclusion, the lessons I have learned over the past twenty-five years about serial killers and sadistic murderers are to some degree time tested. Many of the violent crimes I've researched have had great visibility. The large body counts and extreme brutality ensured that these crimes would make the headlines and be featured on national newscasts. The images of these murderers are easily recognized by millions of ordinary people. Some of the killers' names have become household words; others have provided the inspiration for popular Hollywood films. Criminologists have delved into every detail of their lives, looking for clues and answers.

Because horrendous murders are so high-profile, they often shape public opinion and criminal justice policy. Even a violent crime so extraordinary that it might never happen again can inspire major changes in law and policy. Even a characteristic of a murderer that has nothing to do with motivating him to kill may be latched onto by the public as the cause of his violent behavior. Some suggested changes are beneficial; others make little sense. A few may be so misguided that the effort can only inspire more of the same deadly violence that occurred in the first place.

At the same time, we are not totally in the dark in understanding where sadistic killers get their start or what motivates them to inflict pain and suffering on their victims. As we have seen, they are desperate to achieve a sense of power and control; they come to think of their hideous crimes as their greatest accomplishments. Let us examine their motivations with an eye toward providing alienated individuals—who can possibly be deterred from violent crime—with more constructive ways to lead their lives. In the process, we might also prevent the next mass murder.

NOTES

CHAPTER 1

1. Jack Levin and James Alan Fox, *Mass Murder: America's Growing Menace* (New York: Berkley True Crime, 1991), pp. 122–41.

2. Personal conversation with Kenneth Bianchi, July 1987.

3. "The Mind of a Murderer," *Frontline*, Public Broadcasting System, no. 206, March 1984.

4. Ted Schwartz, *The Hillside Strangler: A Murderer's Mind* (Garden City, NY: Doubleday, 1981).

CHAPTER 2

1. James Alan Fox, Jack Levin, and Kenna Quinet, *The Will to Kill: Making Sense of Senseless Murder*, 3rd ed. (Boston: Allyn and Bacon, 2008).

2. Robert K. Ressler, Ann W. Burgess, and John E. Douglas, *Sexual Homicide: Patterns and Motives* (New York: Lexington Books, 1988).

3. Erich Fromm, *The Anatomy of Human Destructiveness* (New York: Holt, Rinehart, & Winston, 1973).

4. George Gerbner, *Television and Its Viewers: What Social Science Sees* (Santa Monica, CA: Rand Corporation, 1976).

5. Arnold Arluke, Jack Levin, Carter Luke, and Frank Ascione, "The Relationship of Animal Abuse to Violence and Other Forms of Anti-Social Behavior," *Journal of Interpersonal Violence* 14 (1999): 963–75.

6. James Alan Fox and Jack Levin, *Killer on Campus* (New York: Avon Books, 1996).

CHAPTER 3

1. Jan Bouchard-Kerr, Crimelibrary.com, http://www.crimelibrary.com /serial_killers/predators/olsen/1.html.

2. Steven Egger, "Linkage Blindness: A Systemic Myopia," in *Serial Murder: An Elusive Phenomenon*, ed. Steven Egger (New York: Praeger, 1990).

3. M. Gray, "$100,000 Soaked in Blood," *Maclean's*, January 25, 1982, 19–21.

4. Personal conversation, June 1992.

5. "Clifford Olson 'Will Kill Again' If Freed, Parole Board Says in Ruling," CBC News, updated Tuesday, July 18, 2006, http://www.cbc .ca/canada/story/2006/07/18/olsen-hearing.html; "Parole Hearing Being Planned for Clifford Olson," http:// www.ctv.ca/servlet /ArticlNews /story/CTVNews/20060621/olsen_parole_hearing_060621/20060621?hub= Canada, updated June 21, 2006.

CHAPTER 4

1. *The Montel Williams Show*, October 2, 1997.

2. Lisa Price, "Trial Begins against Nurse Charged in 7 Deaths," CNN.com, September 7, 1999, http://www.cnn.com/US/9909/07/indiana .hospitals.deaths.02/index.html.

3. Personal conversation, December 1991.

4. Personal conversation, September 10, 1996.

5. Ibid.·

CHAPTER 5

1. Don Lasseter, *Dead of Night* (New York: Onyx True Crime, 1997).

2. William McCall, "Benetton Anti-Death Penalty Ad Features Four Oregon Killers," Associated Press State & Local Wire, January 21, 2000.

3. Holly Danks, "Cesar Barone, Convicted Killer, Says Detective Is Picking on Him," *Oregonian*, October 2, 1997.

4. Danks, "Prosecutors Fill Canvas with Portrait of Cesar Barone," *Oregonian*, January 31, 1995.

5. Ashbel S. Green, "Court Rejects Appeals from Oregon Pair; Two Murderers Sentenced to Die Continue a Legal Battle for Their Lives," *Oregonian*, January 11, 2000.

CHAPTER 6

1. *The Jerry Springer Show*, September 1995.

2. Jenna Russell, "Slain Woman Was No Hater, Probers Say," *Boston Globe*, February 7, 2006; Katie Zezima, "Teenager Attacks Three Men at Gay Bar in Massachusetts," *New York Times*, February 3, 2006; Pamela H. Sacks, "This Just In . . ." *Worcester Telegram & Gazette*, April 7, 2006.

3. Personal conversation, February 2006.

4. Jack Levin and Arnold Arluke, "Can We Heal Extreme Hate?" *Boston Globe*, August 7, 2006.

5. United States Department of Justice, "Evidence of Magleby's Cross-Burning," 1996, http://www.usdoj.gov/crt/briefs/magleby.htm.

6. Joe Holleman and William C. Lhotka, "Inmate Recounts 20 Murderous Years; Man Says Hatred and Anger Drove Him to Plot, Kill," *St. Louis Post-Dispatch*, June 5, 1995; Kim Bell, "Convicted Killer, Avowed Racist Tells of a Life of Rage, Hatred," *St. Louis Post-Dispatch*, February 2, 1997.

7. James A. Fox, Ann Burgess, Jack Levin, and Alan Burgess, "The Capitol Hill Murders," *Brief Treatment and Crisis Intervention*, May 2007.

8. Ibid.

9. Jack Levin and Jack McDevitt, *Hate Crimes Revisited* (Boulder, CO: Westview Press, 2002); Jack Levin and Gordana Rabrenovic, *Why We Hate* (Amherst, NY: Prometheus Books, 2002).

CHAPTER 7

1. Tom Farmer and Eric Convey, "'Dr. Jekyll' Allegations Stun Medical Community," *Boston Herald*, March 1, 2000.

2. Tom Farmer, "Alleged Murder Weapons Unveiled," *Boston Herald*, May 6, 2001.

3. Mac Daniel, "Greineder Guilty of Murder, Doctor Gets Life Term, No Parole," *Boston Globe*, June 30, 2001.

4. Personal correspondence, May 2007.

CHAPTER 8

1. Charles Wellford and James Cronin, "Clearing Up Homicide Clearance Rates," *National Institute of Justice Journal*, National Institute of Justice, April 2000, pp. 1–7.

2. Earl Ofari Hutchinson, "This Rapper Would Not Snitch on Cho," *New American Media*, April 24, 2007, http://news.newamericamedia.org/news/view_article.html?article_id=b0b4f14c5bd3722f2243ac236a25e16f.

3. "School Gunman Stole Police Pistol, Vest," CNN.com, March 23, 2005, http://www.cnn.com/2005/US/03/22/school.shooting.

4. "Chronology of Smart Murder Case," *Union Leader*, March 23, 1991.

5. Personal conversation, June 2007.

6. Personal correspondence, June 2007.

CHAPTER 9

1. Personal conversation, May 2007.

2. Eli Sagan, *Cannibalism* (New York: Harper Torchbooks, 1981).

3. Personal conversation, September 1991.

4. Personal conversation, October 1991.

CHAPTER 10

1. Deanna Martin, "Police Say Tip Led to Quick Arrest in Sniper Shooting," Associated Press, July 27, 2006.

2. Tony Blais, "Long Trial for Svekla; Jury in Double-Murder Case May

Face Rare Challenge," *Edmonton Sun*, March 17, 2007; Karen Kleiss, "Svekla Murder Trial Set for February," *Edmonton Journal* (Alberta), March 24, 2007.

3. Personal conversation, September 1991.

4. James Alan Fox and Jack Levin, *The Will to Kill: Making Sense of Senseless Murder*, 3rd ed. (Boston: Allyn and Bacon, 2008).

CHAPTER 11

1. Jack Levin and James Alan Fox, *Mass Murder: America's Growing Menace* (New York: Berkley Books, 1991).

2. Telephone conversation with Charles Manson, 2007.

3. *The Geraldo Rivera Show*, November 1991.

4. Edward George, "Chat," *Court TV News*, 2001, http://www.courttv.com/talk/chat_transcripts/manson.html.

5. Ibid.

6. Personal correspondence, May 2007.

7. George, "Chat."

CHAPTER 12

1. Jack Levin, *Domestic Terrorism* (New York: Chelsea House, 2006), pp. 24–26.

2. James Alan Fox, Jack Levin, and Kenna Quinet, *The Will to Kill: Making Sense of Senseless Murder*, 3rd ed. (Boston: Allyn and Bacon, 2008).

3. Paul Farhi and Linton Weeks, "With the Snipers, TV Profilers Missed Their Mark," *Washington Post*, October 25, 2002.

4. Reni Gertner, "Eyewitness Testimony Is Being Challenged More Successfully," *Lawyers USA* (June 29, 2007).

5. Mike Ahlers, "Lawyers Claim Malvo Brainwashed," CNN.com, June 26, 2003.

6. Personal conversation, June 1994.

7. Personal correspondence, May 2007.

8. Ibid.

9. Jack Levin and James Alan Fox, *Mass Murder: America's Growing Menace* (New York: Berkley Books, 1991), pp. 186–91.

10. Personal conversation, June 1994.

11. Personal correspondence, May 2007.

12. Ibid.

13. Personal conversation, July 1991.

CHAPTER 13

1. Michael S. Smith, "Fired Postal Worker Charged with Killing Former Supervisor, 3 Others," Associated Press, October 11, 1991; Don Lasseter, *Going Postal: Madness and Mass Murder in America's Post Offices* (New York: Pinnacle Books, 1997), p. 156.

2. Michelle Koidin, "Killer of Quads' Mother Gets Life," *Star-Ledger*, November 3, 2000.

3. David Kihara, "Police: Slaying Suspect Had Threatened Women," *Las Vegas Review-Journal*, May 31, 2006.

4. Personal conversation and correspondence, October 2006.

5. Paul Hammel, "Friend Doubts Prof Killed Himself," *Omaha World-Herald*, May 10, 2007; Nate Jenkins, "Mystery Swirls around Professor's Fiery Death," Associated Press, May 9, 2007.

6. Personal conversation, September 2006.

CHAPTER 14

1. Personal conversations, October 1996 and May 2007.

2. David Johnston, "17-Year Search, an Emotional Discovery and Terror Ends," *New York Times*, May 5, 1998; Laura Brown, "Classmates Say Math Wiz Didn't Add Up to Much," *Boston Herald*, April 4, 1996; Richard Cole, "Unabomb Manifesto Discovered in Cabin," *Philadelphia Inquirer*, April 13, 1996.

3. Chris Hollis, "Adolescent Schizophrenia," *Advances in Psychiatric Treatment* 6, no. 2 (2000): 83–92.

4. Richard Price, "Unabomber: A Hero to Some," *USA Today*, April 11, 1996.

5. Suzanne Smalley, "Families Hope Evacuation Leads to Closure on Missing Women," *Boston Globe*, May 5, 2007.

6. Ibid.

7. Personal conversation, June 2007.

8. Personal conversations, October 2006 and June 2007.

9. Ibid.

10. Charles M. Sennott, "A Mother on a Mission," *Boston Globe Magazine*, May 13, 2007, 24–27, 34–35.

11. Personal conversation, May 1992.

12. "Whatever Happened to Sylvia Seegrist?" WCAU, June 14, 2006.

13. Ron Word, "Five Years Pass Since Worst Killings in Florida History," *Ledger*, June 19, 1995; Chris Lavin, "Gunman Kills 8, Himself in Jacksonville Auto Loan Office," *St. Petersburg Times*, June 19, 1990; James Alan Fox and Jack Levin, *Extreme Killing: Understanding Serial and Mass Murder* (Thousand Oaks, CA: Sage Publications, 2005), p. 222.

CHAPTER 15

1. Michael S. Smith, "Fired Postal Worker Charged with Killing Former Supervisor, 3 Others," Associated Press, October 11, 1991; Don Lasseter, *Going Postal: Madness and Mass Murder in America's Post Offices* (New York: Pinnacle Books, 1997), p. 156.

2. Erlend Clouston and Sarah Boseley, "Gunman Mows Down Class of Children Leaving 16 Dead with Their Teacher," *Guardian Unlimited*, March 14, 1996.

3. James Alan Fox and Jack Levin, *Killer on Campus* (New York: Avon Books, 1996).

4. Taken from http://www.crimelibrary.com/criminal_mind/forensics/anthropology/1.html.

5. Personal conversation, June 1994.

6. Fox and Levin, *Killer on Campus*.

7. Jack Levin and James Alan Fox, *Mass Murder: America's Growing Menace* (New York: Berkley Books, 1991).

8. Michael Kernan, "The Calamityville Horror," *Washington Post*, September 16, 1979.

CHAPTER 16

1. Sari Horwitz, "Va. Tech Shooter Seen as 'Collector of Injustice,'" *Washington Post*, June 19, 2007.

2. "College Mental Health Study," mtvU, 2006, http://www.halfofus.com/_media/_pr/mtvUCollegeMentalHealthStudy2006.pdf.

3. Margery Eagan, "No Easy Answers on Release, Rehabilitation of Young Killers," *Boston Herald*, May 10, 2004.

4. Robert D. Putnam, *Bowling Alone: The Collapse and Revival of the American Community* (New York: Simon and Schuster, 2000).

CHAPTER 17

1. Donna M. Bishop, Charles E. Frazier, Lonn Lanza-Kaduce, and Lawrence Winner, "The Transfer of Juveniles to Criminal Court: Reexamining Recidivism Over the Long Term," *Crime and Delinquency* 43, no. 4 (October 1997): 240–54.

2. James Alan Fox, Jack Levin, and Kenna Quinet, *The Will to Kill: Making Sense of Senseless Murder*, 3rd ed. (Boston: Allyn and Bacon, 2008), pp. 77–93.

3. Jack Levin, "Keeping an Eye and a Camera on College Students," *Boston Globe*, February 5, 2005.

4. Daniel Macallair, "The Impact of Juvenile Curfew Laws in California," Center on Juvenile and Criminal Justice, 2002, http://www.cjcj.org/pubs/curfew/curfew.html.

5. Jack Levin, "Keeping Children Safe from Sex Crimes," *Boston Globe*, July 18, 2005.

6. David Abel, "Many Sex Offenders End Up at Shelters," *Boston Globe*, June 18, 2007.

7. Stephen M. Silverman, "Martha: My Prison Nickname Was M. Diddy," http://www.people.com/people/article/0,,1079743,00.html.

8. Richard C. Dieter, "Costs of the Death Penalty and Related Issues," Judiciary Committee of the Colorado House of Representatives, Denver, Colorado, February 7, 2007; "Attitudes Toward the Death Penalty for Persons Convicted of Murder," Department of Justice, *Sourcebook of Criminal Justice Statistics Online*, 2006, www.albany.edu/sourcebook/pdf.

9. Dane Archer and Rosemary Gartner, *Violence and Crime in Cross-National Perspective* (New Haven, CT: Yale University Press, 1984).

10. William J. Bowers, *Executions in America* (Lexington, MA: Lexington Books, 1974).

11. Jeffrey Fagan, "Deterrence and the Death Penalty," testimony to the New York State Assembly Committee on Codes, January 21, 2005.

12. Ibid.

INDEX

.